HIJAB BUTCH BLUES

HIJAB BUTCH BLUES

A Memoir

Lamya H

THE DIAL PRESS | NEW YORK

Hijab Butch Blues is a work of memoir. It is a true story based on the author's best recollections of various events in her life. In some instances, events and time periods have been compressed or reordered in service of the narrative and dialogue approximated to match the author's best recollections of those exchanges. Names and identifying details have been changed.

Copyright © 2023 by Lamya H

Published in the United States by The Dial Press, an imprint of Random House, a division of Penguin Random House LLC, New York.

THE DIAL PRESS is a registered trademark and the colophon is a trademark of Penguin Random House LLC.

Hardback ISBN 9780593448762
Ebook ISBN 9780593448779

Printed in Canada on acid-free paper

randomhousebooks.com

2 4 6 8 9 7 5 3 1

First Edition

Book design by Susan Turner

For my beloved family, chosen and bio.
For J.

CONTENTS

PREFACE

*And when Ibrahim said, "My Lord, show me how You
give life to the dead."
[Allah] said, "Have you not believed?"
[Ibrahim] said, "Yes, but just that my heart may be
satisfied."*
—*The Quran, 2:260*

This is my favorite verse in the Quran. Even Ibrahim, a
prophet who talks to God, who has received revelations and
miracles—even this prophet has doubts. He turns to God
and asks gingerly, *Will You really bring me back to life when
I am dead? I believe in You, God, but there's a part of me that
is unsure. My heart hesitates. My mind has questions. And I
can't help but ask them.*

    I, too, have questions for God—when I'm falling in love
with a woman, when I'm figuring out my gender, when I

move to the U.S. for college away from everyone I know and can't make sense of why I feel so wrong. Like Ibrahim, I, too, can't help but turn to God with my questions, my doubts, my anger, my love. Like Ibrahim, I, too, hope that my heart may be satisfied.

PART
I

MARYAM

I.

I am fourteen the year I read Surah Maryam. It's not like I haven't read this chapter of the Quran before, I have—I've read the entire Quran multiple times, all 114 chapters from start to finish. But I've only read it in Arabic, a language that I don't speak, that I can vocalize but not understand, that I've been taught for the purpose of reading the Quran. So I've read Surah Maryam before: sounded out the letters, rattled off words I don't know the meaning of, translated patterns of print into movements of tongue and lips. Read as an act of worship, an act of learning, an act of obedience to my father, under whose supervision I speed-read two pages of Quran aloud every evening. I've heard the surah read, too—recited on the verge of song during Taraweeh prayer in Ramadan; on the Quran tapes we listen to in the car during traffic jams; on the Islamic radio station that blares in the background while my mother cooks. This surah is beautiful, and one that I'm intimately familiar with. The cadence of its internal rhyme, the five elongated letters that comprise the first verse, the short, hard consonants repeated in intervals. But although I've read Surah Maryam before, my appreciation for it has been limited to the ritual and the aesthetic. I've never *read* read it.

I am fourteen the year we read Surah Maryam in Quran class. We, as in the twenty-odd students in my grade, in the girls' section of the Islamic school that I attend in this rich Arab country that my family has moved to. It's not a fancy international school, but my classmates and I are from all over the world—Bangladesh, Nigeria, Egypt, Germany— and our parents are always telling us to be grateful for our opportunities. Mine are always reminding me why we left the country I was born in a decade ago—a country where we lived next door to my grandmother and a few streets down from my cousins, where I remember being surrounded by love—to this country where we don't know anyone and don't know the language and my mother can't drive. My parents are always listing reasons we've stayed: better jobs, more stability, a Muslim upbringing. Which includes an Islamic education in school.

Twice a week, my classmates and I have Quran class. We line up in the windowless hallway outside the room where we have most of our other lessons—a room we've decorated and claimed desks in and settled into. From there, we begrudgingly make our way to a drab room in the annex called the "language lab." The name is deceptive; it's just a regular classroom outfitted with headphones and tape players, recently appropriated from the boys' section in an attempt at a more equal distribution of the school's resources. But gross boy smells—sweat and farts and cheap deodorant—still linger in the windowless room, and it's a five-minute walk away on the other side of the school's campus. Understandably, the rate of attrition is high for these trips to Quran class. Girls duck out to the bathroom along the way and fail to rejoin the procession ("Miss, I really have to change my pad, but I'll be right back, wallah"), or feign ignorance of where class is being held ("Miss, someone told us the language lab is closed this week so we waited in our classroom the entire time"), or pretend to have gotten lost ("Miss, I really thought I had to take a right at the stairs and by the time I figured it out, it didn't make sense to disturb the lesson"). It is unbelievably easy to skip Quran class.

I, on the other hand, never skip Quran class. I go to every single one without fail, not because of religious devoutness, but because that's the kind of ninth grader I am. Too scared to cut class and a terrible liar. An overachiever, hell-bent on getting good grades and ranking first in my class. A nerd, hungry to learn about anything and everything; an avid reader, fascinated by the storytelling aspect of Quran class and eager to know what happens next; a clown, unwilling to give up having an audience for the jokes and convoluted questions and inappropriate remarks that I offer in class, preferring the laughs and groans and eye rolls of my classmates to being with myself, to the thoughts that pulse through my solitude.

But also, there's this: I'm bored. I'm thoroughly bored by school. I've figured out that each class contains only about ten minutes of actual learning that I need to pay attention to at the start of the period, and then I can tune out. I've figured out that my teachers are puzzles that can be cracked with a little effort at the beginning of the semester: which teachers reward acting like you're trying hard, which ones have soft spots for quick-witted students, which ones just want everyone to be quiet in class. I've figured this out: once I listen for a bit in class and grasp the new material and win over the teacher, I can spend the rest of the time doing whatever I want. Sometimes this means decorating my pencil case with correction fluid; other times it means reading contraband novels under my desk. Sometimes it means disrupting the class: coming up with pointed questions of existential importance that I just *need* to ask the teacher now. But mostly, it means whispering with—and distracting—whoever ends up sitting next to me.

This Quran class is no different. We are slogging through Surah Maryam painfully slowly, about ten verses at a time. The only part of class I enjoy is the beginning. We start by listening to the recitation of the verses in Arabic. One of the girls in my class is a Quran aficionado and brings in tapes of reciters with lush, melodious voices. I put on my head-phones, close my eyes, and for a few minutes let the sounds wash over me. I lose myself to the tune set by the rhyme, I let myself be moved. This part always comes to an end too soon. The teacher stops the tape and takes over, reading the verses one by one in a stoic monotone, each word clear and well enunciated. And we follow, mimicking her tone and reciting lazily, most of us just mumbling through and letting the Arab girls who know what they're doing take up the bulk of the aural space.

The next part of class is the translation. We read the English meaning of the Arabic words we've just recited, with everyone taking turns reading one verse aloud from our government-issued Qurans. I deliberately sit near the back of the class so we'll be done reading before my turn comes, so I can skim through the translation of the verses we've read and then blissfully tune out the rest of the lesson. Today I'm composing a note on my calculator to my best friend, with whom I've been trying to come up with a code using numbers and symbols and the smattering of letters on the keyboards of our scientific calculators—then someone in the first row reads the translation of this verse aloud:

And the pains of childbirth [of Isa] drove her [Maryam]
to the trunk of a palm tree. She said, "Oh, I wish I
had died before this and was in oblivion, forgotten."
(19:23)

I stop writing my note, stop looking at my watch, stop trying to decide what I'll eat for lunch, stop breathing for a second. Because this verse is saying that Maryam wants to die. Maryam, of the eponymous surah we're reading, wants to die. Maryam—who has a whole chapter devoted to her in the Quran, this woman beloved to God, the mother of a prophet, held up as an example to mankind—is saying she wants to die. In this difficult moment of childbirth, of birthing the prophet Isa, who will go on to birth the entire religion of Christianity, this Maryam is talking to God, complaining to God, screaming in pain to God that she wants to be in oblivion, forgotten. That she wants to die.

II.

I am fourteen the year I want to die. Nothing has happened to precipitate this feeling, but that's part of the problem: nothing happens in my life. I live in this country my parents moved us to when I was four and my brother was two— away from everything and everyone we knew. Nothing happens here, but I suppose that's part of the draw for my parents: no political upheavals, no wars, all of which they've lived through back home.

Nothing happens in this country and nothing happens in my life, this life I've never had a choice in. Not in having been born, not in having been moved, and certainly not in the mundanities of my everyday. I wake up in the morning. I go to school. I study the subjects that were chosen for me by virtue of my good grades. I come home. I do chores, I do homework, I go to bed. I can't go anywhere without my parents because there is no other way to leave the house, no public transport, no method of travel that doesn't involve my father driving. When we go out as a family, it is mostly to dinner parties at my parents' friends' houses: stuffy affairs segregated by gender and age where the other teenagers both bore me and ignore me. We come back from these parties and I brush my teeth and go to sleep and wake up and repeat all these actions to prepare for a future that I never asked for, the days blending into each other in a life that I never asked for, this life that's never been my own.

So I want to die. Not dramatically, not in some big performative way—although sometimes I cannot stop thinking about the beauty of cutting myself. How satisfying it would be to run a razor down my arm in two sharp nicks length-wise; how satisfying it would be to watch the tracks left by the blade fill slowly with blood and spill over. The splendor of this image, red trails down my forearms, would be the last thing I'd see before fading out.

But I don't actually want to die like that, and I don't want to die tragically, either, in the myriad ways I can think of. Not from cancer or some other fast-acting terminal disease. I don't want that kind of attention, my body wasting, my friends wailing, people visiting to ask for forgiveness, people saying their final goodbyes. I don't want to die painfully, nor by deliberate accident. Not hit by a car that I've thrown myself in front of, not falling out of a roller coaster where I've forgotten to wear a seatbelt, not slipping through a window I've intentionally left unlatched. I don't want to die in any of these ways that would leave people grieving, would leave behind shock waves and melancholy and the certainty of pain for others.

What I want instead is to disappear. Stop living, more like. I just want to stop being alive. It's a constant ache, this wanting to disappear. A craving that's always there, even when I'm with my friends, even when I'm outwardly joking around or playing games or making people laugh. Even when I'm doing things that have previously brought me pleasure, even in situations where I look like I'm having fun. I just don't want to do this thing called living anymore, and this feeling both creates and fills up an emptiness inside me. I want my parents never to have had me, I want my friends never to have known me, I want none of this life I never asked for. I want never to have lived at all.

So I practice disappearing, I practice disappearing all the time: at home, at school, at a dinner party my parents drag me to one Friday night—a wedding anniversary celebration for their friends. I'm sitting with the women and girls in an ornate living room where we're curtained from the men so everyone can remove their hijabs, and I'm immeasurably bored. The other girls my age go to a different high school, and I have nothing to add to their rambunctious conversation about teachers, cafeteria food, and how to sneak makeup past their draconian monitors. Everyone else—the married women, including my mother, who is a few seats away—is engaged in a lively discussion about making samosas using frozen spring roll wrappers. I don't want to be here, all dressed up in an itchy sequined shalwar kameez that my mother insisted I wear. I'd do anything to be anywhere but here, sitting in this living room among these people who are talking, eating, happy.

My mother gets up to refill her plate and stoops beside me, outwardly smiling as she whispers angrily in my ear, "Lamya, you need to talk to the other girls. Can you at least try to have fun?"

The only way I could have fun at this dinner party is if I wasn't here, so I decide to make that happen. I spot a mirror on the opposite wall, where everyone else in the reflection is talking, eating, happy. I position myself near a corner of the reflection and slowly edge myself out. Slowly move out of the frame inch by inch, to the left at first and then down, slouching lower and lower on my chair so I'm no longer in the reflection and the scene is left intact. Looking at the scene in the mirror—everyone else still gathered, talking, eating, happy—makes me feel strangely relieved. As if these people never knew me, as if I had never come to this party, as if I had never been born.

I practice disappearing with my friends, too. At school, on the bus, at a mall one evening that my friend bribes her brother to drive us to. None of us are ever able to go any-where—we never have rides—and going to the mall by our-selves feels like we've lucked into a treat. We get to spend three whole hours together without our parents around, three hours to do whatever we want, three hours of some-thing approaching freedom. My friends and I are giddy; we've been planning this outing for weeks. But when it fi-nally happens, all they want to do is go into stores and try on clothes, shoes, and jewelry. I follow them around obediently until suddenly, I want to be anywhere but there, I want to disappear. So I grow quiet slowly over the course of the eve-ning, lowering the volume of my voice by a fraction of a decibel every time I speak, until I'm saying things that are barely audible, until I'm saying things that no one notices, until finally I'm saying nothing, sometimes moving my lips but mostly doing nothing at all.

I try to go the entire evening without anyone noticing that I'm not talking, and I almost get away with it. But then, at the end of our allotted time, we're waiting in the parking lot for my friend's brother to pick us up, when one of my friends says something.

"Lamya, are you okay? It's not like you to be so quiet."

"Yeah. I'm fine." Embarrassingly, my voice croaks from disuse, but I'm secretly pleased that my desire for disap-pearing is manifesting in physical ways.

"Are you sure?"

"Yeah. How are *you* doing, though? You haven't updated us in a while about that boy you have a crush on."

My friend squeals, happy to talk about this boy who lives in her building, whom she gets to talk to for a few minutes every morning while they're waiting for their respective school buses. I know I should be sad at how easy it is to deflect her question, but that's not what I feel. I don't really feel anything; I haven't felt anything in months. It's fascinating how busy my friends are with being the center of their own worlds. And my parents have never been very involved or perceptive of my inner life. I get good grades and I don't act up, so they've never needed to understand me—unlike my brother, who gets mediocre grades and struggles with making friends, and therefore gets all of their focus and attention and energy. (Decades later, my mother will throw out a casual remark about how easy I was as a teenager and I'll be shocked anew that she never knew, that she never even tried to know.) Once in a while, when people notice that I'm less of myself and ask if I'm okay, I tell them yes, of course everything is okay. I don't tell anyone that I'm tired of living, that I'm hungry to disappear.

Partly because I don't know it myself: I don't have words for this feeling, just nebulous thoughts about this thing that is not talked about in my family, my culture, in Islam. My mother's cousin is found dead in his college dorm room when I'm really young, and even years later there's a deafening hush around his death. *Who knows what happened,* everyone says. *It could have been anything—heart attack, stroke—no one knows what happened, he just died, that's all.*

The intensity of the ensuing hush swallows all questions. Suicide, we're told once in a while in Friday sermons, Islam classes, halaqa reading circles, is the work of the devil. It's cowardly, one of the biggest sins, punishable by hell, takes one out of the fold of Islam, means no funeral prayer, no Muslim burial, *audhubillahi minnash shaytan arrajeem*. But that's not what I'm struggling with, I tell myself; that's not what this is. And it's not, not really; these feelings that I'm having, that I'm hiding, are different. I just want to erase myself retroactively. Like Maryam, I don't want to kill myself, I want to be in oblivion, forgotten. I want to die.

III.

Maryam has had it rough. It's no wonder she wants to die. Her life was decided for her before she was born. Her mother, pregnant with a child she's convinced is a boy, dedicates the baby to God. Maryam's mother swears an oath to the Divine, turns to the heavens and gives her unborn son to a life in service of God. *This child is Yours,* she tells God. *This child will worship You, will live a small life, a simple life, a quiet life in Your mosque, will spend his life serving those who worship You.* And God accepts this gift.

And then Maryam is born, born a girl, born wrong. Her mother is distraught, laments: What did I do to deserve this, to have birthed a girl? A girl who cannot live by herself, who cannot protect herself, who is now pledged to the mosque, who is now pledged to God? But God is the best of planners, tells Maryam's mother not to worry, that her gift is accepted, that Maryam has been chosen for the service of God.

So Maryam spends the first few years of her life in her mother's house, with her family—just a few years, not a lot. Long enough to learn to take care of herself, to learn how to survive. Long enough to love and be loved by her siblings, by her mother, her father, this child who was always destined to leave. Long enough for it to hurt when she leaves, this child born a girl, born wrong, whose life was never her own.

Then one day when Maryam is old enough, she is taken to the mosque where she is to spend the rest of her life. All alone, a child still, she is to spend her life in constant devotion to God: praying salah and fasting and reciting dhikr. And between these acts of worship, she is to maintain the mosque: sweeping and dusting and cleaning and refilling the water urns. All day, every day these routine tasks. No one for company except stray wanderers, and once in a while, her uncle Zakariya, who only visits because he has to. He has lost the drawing of lots for who has to take care of Maryam, when the men of the family fought among themselves not to have to be responsible for her, to bring her food, and to check in on her once in a while.

Maryam settles into this life alone and far from everyone she loves. She's made peace with herself and her circumstances, and finds herself loving this worship, this solitude, this closeness to God. And God is good to her. God keeps her safe and protects her and feeds her with fruit sent from the heavens, trays laden with more food than she can eat that just appear on her doorstep—until. (Always, there is a turn, an until.)

Until God sends an angel to tell Maryam, *Hello, guess what, you're pregnant. You have been chosen and you're going to have a child. Not just any child—a prophet. Prophet Isa, in fact. Jesus. A prophet who will go on to lead billions, who will found the entire religion of Christianity—this is the prophet who is growing inside you.* Maryam is a teenager in most versions of this story. She's still a kid, this Maryam, she's never had sex with a man. She lives on her own and prays all day, away from all her people, away from men, and suddenly there's a child growing inside of her. And not just any child, but a prophet. Maryam's life was never her own, and now neither is her body. It is God's vessel to carry a child she never asked for.

Maryam bears it, of course. What else can one do when chosen by God? Maryam's body grows bigger, expands and distends. There is no mother to watch over her, no coterie of women to take care of her, advise her, answer her questions about the aches and soreness and swelling—the numerous ways in which her body is changing. And as Maryam grows bigger, she also becomes mortified. It's hard to hide her pregnancy, and she understands enough of the world to know that no one will believe that God put this child inside of her. She is embarrassed at what people will assume happened while she was alone in the mosque, what they will say about her character, her family. So when she gets too big to hide her condition, Maryam leaves the mosque that is her whole world. She sneaks away from her small, simple, quiet life and goes somewhere far away in the desert to give birth. Alone. Always alone.

And that's where we are with Maryam in Quran class.

With this child who is with child, giving birth alone under a tree in the middle of the desert. She's in ripping, searing pain like she's never known before. And she is entirely alone. No midwife to remind her to breathe, no mother who has gone through this before to comfort her, no attendant to see to her needs. Maryam is hungry and thirsty and tired. She's angry, too, and she knows that this birth, this agonizing pain of labor, all of this is the easy part. The harder part is yet to come, when she will go back into town and face her people with a baby in her arms. What will they say about her, about this baby and where it came from? Who will believe her when she says it's an act of God? What will they do to her? It is all terrifying, so she turns to the heavens, to God, in pain and, maybe for the first time in her life, in rage. For all that she's been through and borne, for all the ways she's been wrong and wronged, for all the ways in which her life has never been her own, she screams, *Oh, I wish I had died before this and was in oblivion, forgotten.*

She's had it rough, Maryam. Of course she wants to die.

IV.

I am fourteen the year I realize I am gay.

Realize is a strong word. It's not exactly something I realize in the conventional sense; it's not a sudden epiphany, or even something I have language for yet. It's more of a steady gathering of information, a piling up of block upon block until suddenly a tower appears. A tower that is no longer part of the background, a tower that—unlike a scattered set of blocks—is no longer ignorable. And gay is a strong word, too, and not one that I know yet to use for myself. Gay is a hush-hush thing, not to be talked about seriously, only to be used as an insult. What I'm noticing in myself, though I don't quite have the word for this, either, is desire.

I find myself fascinated with this person who happens to be a woman, an economics teacher at my school. She's Irish, in her early thirties, has two boys, and an Arab husband. Rumors of marital discord and an air of tragedy surround her. And also, she is beautiful. Has long blond hair that she never ties back, wears fashionable dresses cut to show unexpected slivers of skin. Her smile is difficult to extract but worth it for the way it spreads across her face, the way that it crinkles her eyes. She is always put together, always precisely on time, thorough in her lessons, and impossible to stump with questions.

But that's all I know about her. She is annoyingly private. Refuses to answer even mundane questions like *How old are your kids, what neighborhood do you live in, what's your favorite kind of food, what books do you read?* She proves to be entirely undistractable and exasperatingly efficient with her lessons. I try really hard to figure her out, and that's how my fascination starts. She is a challenge. The more she brushes off my questions, the more questions I come up with. The more unreadable she is, the more I want to know her, the more I want to decode her. My straight A's in her class don't get her attention. My sitting in the front row doesn't get her attention. My extra reading, my asking thoughtful, difficult questions about the subject matter doesn't get her attention. Nothing works.

So I take to pranking her instead. Slip a tablespoon of salt in her coffee when she steps out for a five-minute break in the middle of a double lesson. She spits the coffee out, makes a face, and laughs tightly. Usually she has a great sense of humor, but she's very serious about her coffee. She is definitely not amused by the "note from my mother" I hand her—it's a contraption that sets off a paper clip/elastic band/cardboard cacophony when opened, resulting in a loud buzz and eliciting a loud scream. She is livid when I put petroleum jelly all over the door handle that leads into our classroom, so she both can't get in and ends up with a sticky, gooey mess on her hands that she has to run to the bathroom to wash off. The other girls in my class are de-lighted. I've never been more popular, more frequently stopped in the hallways, sometimes even by the cool girls, for conversations and ideas for pranks. Everyone thinks I can't stand this teacher, a convenient story that I don't chal-lenge. I can't have anyone know that's not true, that all I want is for her to look at me, to notice me even a fraction of the amount that I notice her.

I'm not even sure what I'd do with her attention, let alone what I want it for. I'm filled with questions, not an-swers. What is her life like? What does she do when she's not teaching? What makes her so sad? I just want to be near her, converse with her, be there for her and her sadness. She makes me feel all these confusing things that I've never felt before. A warmth when she's around, this weird feeling that starts somewhere underneath my rib cage and dries out my tongue and dampens my palms. A hyperawareness of her coordinates at all times, like there's a long invisible string connecting us. A yearning to be seen by her. And this tin-gling, this weird sense of pleasure in parts of myself where I've never felt anything before.

Whatever this is, I do know it feels a lot like what my friends say they feel for boys—this wanting to be near, want-ing to touch, wanting some sort of connection, some inti-macy. I'm good at pretending; I play along with my friends when they talk about feeling these things for boys. Of course, I say, of course I feel these things, too. There's this one boy who lives a few doors down who is appropriately a few years older, and I tell everyone who will listen that I feel these feelings for him. But it's not true, I don't feel that way about him. I don't want him to look at me the way my friends want their crushes to look at them. I don't want to dress up for him, or talk to him or about him for hours. And I defi-nitely do not want to do any of the things my friends tell me I should be doing to get his attention.

It's because I don't feel anything like that for him, or for any boy, really. And why would I? Boys are stupid and smelly and I play sports with them on my street every evening, so I know their world well. I can't stand their posturing and their dumb jokes about how they're better than girls, can't stand the way they don't have to help out with everyday chores, can't stand how much they get away with just because they're boys. I'm friends with them, these boys. I hang out with them all the time, but I don't feel anything resembling the feelings other girls describe. Until I find myself having these feelings for this older woman, this teacher.

Even without words like gay and lesbian and queer, I know instinctively that these feelings are wrong, out of place somehow. These all-consuming feelings that make me see this woman when I close my eyes to sleep at night, that make me find ways to casually inject her into every conversation I have with my friends, that make me so curious about her—whatever these feelings are, I know I must keep them to myself and never share. That's what I tell myself on the good days. On bad days, I am embarrassed at my reactions, mortified at how my body responds to the presence of this woman. I am acutely ashamed. All year that I've been having these feelings, not a day goes by that I am not terrified that someone will find out, paranoid that people can see through me, to this core of me that is wretched and wrong. I feel more alone than I ever have. I don't want this, I don't want to live like this. I want to die.

V.

The week after reading about Maryam wanting to die, I look forward to the next Quran class. I'm jittery as the time approaches, and eager to start walking to the language lab. As usual, my class of twenty-two girls whittles down to a little more than half as we wind our way through the school building to the annex on the other side of campus. The other girls are unhurried when we get there. They take their time choosing seats and chattering and settling, but I'm fast: notebook out, pen out, headphones on, ready to start the lesson. I'm jumpy. Hyperaware of everyone and everything, anxious that I'm being transparent, that everyone can tell that I'm craving the next installment of the story of Maryam, that I'm leaning in so as not to miss a word, that I'm grasping at everything I can learn about this woman who complains to God and wants to die.

But today is a review lesson, the Quran teacher tells us, to prep for our midterm the week after. I'm devastated. I'll have to wait an entire week to know what happens next while we recap the thirty or so verses we've already read, and then review the recitation, the hard words, and the English translation for our upcoming test. Someone in the front row starts reading the beginning of the surah aloud and I sigh, slip into my usual half-listening mode. I nudge my best friend sitting next to me and ask to borrow her multicolored pens for doodling—then someone reads the translation of these verses aloud:

> *And mention in the Book [the story of] Maryam, when she withdrew from her family to a place toward the east.*
> *And she took, in seclusion from them, a screen. Then We sent to her Our angel, and he represented himself to her as a well-proportioned man.*
> *She said, "Indeed, I seek refuge in the Most Merciful from you, [so leave me], if you should be fearing of Allah."*
> *He said, "I am only the messenger of your Lord to give you [news of] a pure boy [Isa]."*
> *She said, "How can I have a boy while no man has touched me . . ." (19:17–19)*

I stop. Stop doodling, stop calculating how many minutes till the end of class, stop thinking about the bag of
chips in my backpack, stop breathing for a second, my body
caught in a moment of clarity that shoots through me and
suspends my thoughts. Suddenly, my arm raises of its own
accord, and before I'm aware of making any conscious decision, I'm speaking, my voice higher than usual and breath-
less. "Miss. Miss. Did Maryam say that no man has touched
her because she didn't like men?"

There is a pause. Two seconds of shocked silence before
my classmates break into titters. Some roll their eyes. This
sounds a lot like one of my infamous questions that derail
the class, and some of my classmates are annoyed that I've
interrupted their get-out-of-jail-free summary of the classes
they've skipped and the things they need to know for the
midterm. But I am grateful, so grateful for the tittering. It
conceals my earnestness. I'm grateful for my earlier antics,
that I get to play off this question as a moment of clowning
instead of a sincere, burning desire for an answer. I need to
know: Is this a thing? Are there other women like me, who
don't like men? Who would tell a handsome, well-
proportioned man-angel who appeared before them to go
away? Who have never been touched by men? Who don't
want to be touched by men?

The Quran teacher, a matronly Sudanese woman in her
sixties who has always been kind to me, doesn't seem to
read anything into my question, and mercifully she does not
skip a beat in her answer.

"No," she says. "It's because Maryam had taqwa, she

had God consciousness in its highest state of being. It's because Maryam was pious and loved and feared God. She knew that the Divine was watching her even if no one else was around, knew that the presence of God was everywhere even if she couldn't see God. Maryam didn't want the privacy of her situation to tempt her into doing something with this beautiful man, something God wouldn't be happy with. Isn't that an excellent lesson to learn, girls? Don't ever forget that God is watching. When you're around boys, God is always watching. If you're alone with a boy, God is watching. If it's just the two of you somewhere, then God is the third. Remember Maryam, girls. Maryam turned to God. She asked the man to go away because she had taqwa."

But I know. I know differently.

VI.

Maryam is a dyke.

Isn't it obvious? Doesn't it make sense? She lives alone in a mosque with no one else around, no one to monitor what she does or whom she meets up with, and not a person in the world for company. One day, a handsome and well-proportioned man comes to her door unannounced. No one will know if he stays awhile, no one will know what they do together. But before he can even talk, Maryam asks him to leave. *No, thank you,* she says, *please don't talk to me.* She would rather have her solitude than the company of this handsome man. Eventually, she lets him stay—but only because he says he's an angel. She hears him out because he's an emissary from God. Laughs heartily when he tells her she's going to have a baby. *Who, me?* she says. *No man has ever touched me. No* man.

And I know, I know she was pious. I know that she was always aware that God was watching. But there's no hesitation, not even for a second, when she turns him down and bars him from her space. It must be because Maryam doesn't like men. Not handsome ones, not well-proportioned ones—these things don't even register for her. No man has ever touched her, she says. She hasn't let them, she hasn't been interested. Maryam is a dyke.

Or maybe she isn't, who knows—dyke isn't even part of my vocabulary at fourteen, and maybe I'm reading too much into this story, these few lines of a text that's been around for fourteen hundred years. But what I do know is this: Maryam is *something,* somehow like me. I feel different that day after Quran class. Relieved, at first, after the embarrassment dies down, after I'm done playing off the question as intentional, after I'm done receiving high fives in the hallways from my classmates for my joke. I'm relieved that no one has caught on and I'm relieved that I'm not the only one like this. And after this relief comes elation. There are other women like me in the Quran. Women who are uninterested in men, who are born wrong, living lives that are entirely out of their control. Women who rage, rage to God no less, about wanting to die.

It's so acute, this elation, that it spills out of my body and into everything. I'm bouncy and chatty the rest of the day; all my classes and interactions feel joyous. My bus ride back from school is joyous, and when I get home, even my lunch is joyous: my mother has spent all day making me meat-free nihari, and I know this is a truce flag in our fights about my recent vegetarianism, which itself is also joyous. The elation grows and grows, and it hurts how much I want to tell someone, anyone, about my joy, maybe even my mother, to whom I never tell anything. I find myself wondering if I should I tell her over lunch about Quran class, about what I've discovered about Maryam, maybe what I've discovered about myself.

But I hesitate. Just for a second, and in that second, my mother sits me down at the lunch table, hands me a plate, and doles out a large portion of stew. She must have noticed my joy, but misreads its source. Looks at the steaming hot bowlful of the meatless version of my favorite food in front of me and smiles. "Don't worry, Lamya," she says. "We'll find you a vegetarian husband."

A what?

Her words puncture the joyousness of the day and my elation steadily seeps out. I will myself to press my lips together tightly, close my mouth so nothing will escape, but it's too late, I've already said it, and emphatically, too. "I'm never going to marry a man, Mama."

My mother laughs and doesn't skip a beat in her answer. "Of course you will. Everyone does. How will you live if you don't get married? Who will take care of you? Who will love you then?"

I clam up, my joy entirely deflated. I don't say anything to my mother in response, just eat my vegetarian nihari in silence. Usually this is when I'd start wanting to disappear, start wanting to die, but something feels different that day.

Something has changed, something entirely new feels possible. I stay quiet, but I'm buzzing on the inside. I want to find out the answer to my mother's questions, not just for myself, but for Maryam, too. How did she live? Who took care of her? Who loved her then? And me. How will I live, how will I create a life for myself? Who will take care of me, who will I take care of? I'm curious about these questions, and curiosity is not compatible with boredom or a desire to disappear.

I am fourteen the year I read Surah Maryam. The year I choose not to die. The year I choose to live.

JINN

I.

It's late—later than I, at seven, have ever been allowed to stay up on a school night. My parents are at a holiday party for my dad's work and they've dropped me and my brother off at Asma Aunty's house for the evening. Asma Aunty doesn't have the same rules as other grown-ups: she lets us stay up late and eat ice cream on her couch. She always has the best stash of toys and movies and snacks even though she doesn't have any kids, which makes her the favorite of my mother's friends. Tonight, after my parents leave, she puts on *Aladdin* as my brother and I jump up and down and cheer.

"Wait," she says, hitting pause on the remote as the opening scene begins. "You're not going to be scared, right?"

"No way," I say. "We're big kids now!"

"We've seen it before! We know that things like genies and magic are pretend!" my brother chimes in.

"But genies aren't pretend," Asma Aunty says. My brother and I stare at her, eyes as big as the chips we're eating. She looks back at us, just as astonished as we are. "Are you telling me no one has ever told you a jinn story?"

My brother and I shake our heads and put down the bowl of chips, eager to catch every word.

"Aladdin doesn't count as a real jinn story," she says. "Jinns are not blue and they don't live in lamps—that's just in the cartoon. But jinns are real beings, just like you and me. They're part of the ghaib, which are the unseen things in Islam that we have to believe in without seeing, like the angels and hellfire. They're everywhere around us—watching us quietly, listening to things we say, and living among us in the world." My brother and I look around the room curiously, trying to spot any jinn we might have missed in a corner, or sitting on one of the other chairs.

"Usually you can't see jinn, but sometimes they can change their shape into something that you can see, like an animal or an old woman." Asma Aunty pauses. "Oh, God, I can't believe I'm telling you your first jinn story; your mom is going to kill me. But it's important that you know all of this!" My brother and I look at each other, wordlessly promising not to tell our mom.

Asma Aunty scoots closer to us. "The thing is: jinn are evil. They're always making trouble for people. And they can fly." She pauses, then says in a low voice, "I saw a jinn once. It took the shape of a black cat. I almost didn't see it at first. It was night and I was walking to our car that, of course, your uncle Hadi had parked in the darkest part of the grocery store lot. Then I saw it. This cat was slinking around, invisible in the dark except for a pair of green eyes that were looking right at me. It stopped and stared at me, and slowly I saw the rest of its dark body. Its fur was matted and it was caked in dirt. I was so scared that both my arms broke out in goosebumps. I knew something was weird about this cat, so I got into the car quickly and ordered Hadi to drive us home as fast as he could. For the whole ten-minute drive, I was shaking with fear. When we finally got to our building, I opened the door, and guess what was sitting there, right in the bushes? A pair of green eyes. The same cat, dirty and covered in mud. It had followed us home. I screamed so loud that some of the neighbors opened their windows to see what was going on. The cat was obviously a jinn, because that's what jinn do, they disappear and then appear out of nowhere to cause problems. Wait, why are you both crying? Don't be scared. Most of the time we can't even see jinn. They're invisible! You'll forget that they're even there!"

For weeks afterward, my brother and I have nightmares about that cat.

II.

There are lots of cool things about Rasha. For one, she's in the fifth grade—two whole grades older than me—and she has pink highlights in her blond hair. She always has the newest sneakers and goes to the cool French lycée that all the rich Arab kids, who look down on my Islamic school,

attend. But the coolest thing about Rasha is that she has a
pogo stick.

My brother and I have been eyeing this pogo stick for
weeks. Every day, an hour before Maghrib prayer, Rasha
brings the pogo stick down to the park behind our apartment building, and every day my brother and I watch Rasha
from the corner where we play. She doesn't know we exist,
but because we've been eyeing this pogo stick, we know all
these things about Rasha. We know that she starts her pogo
stick practice session every day by jumping one hundred
times without stopping. We know she has rapidly been getting better: beats everyone in timed runs and has taught
herself to jump over small obstacles. A few days ago, we
watched from afar as all the other Arab kids stood in a circle
and cheered her jumping a thousand times in a row. Rasha's
brother, who is in third grade like me, sometimes plays with
the pogo stick, too. He's not as good or as steady at jumping
as Rasha, but he's fast at getting around the playground and
kind of scary. He hollers and chases down other kids while
he jumps, but is ultimately better at terrorizing the playground on his feet, so he doesn't use the pogo stick very
much. Rasha, on the other hand, is doggedly consistent.

My brother and I want a pogo stick badly, but we're too
shy to ask to use Rasha's and too shy to ask our parents to
buy us one. We talk about this dilemma every day. After a
detailed debate weighing the pros and cons of both options,
we decide to ask our parents to buy us a pogo stick: less
scary, higher chance of success. We reason that the best
time to bring up our proposition is when our parents will be

most relaxed and amenable to our pleas (after dinner). We use rock-paper-scissors to pick who will do the talking (my brother). We write out what we're going to say, then practice saying it aloud. We run through my parents' possible responses and map out counterarguments.

Finally, we muster every last bit of our collective courage and, over the remains of chicken pulao on the dinner table, we make our appeal. The table falls silent. We don't ask for things often, and there are a few moments after our request when it seems like we've surprised our parents into saying yes. But then my mother, who walks us over to the playground every day and sits on a bench and reads the Quran while we play, who watches us watching Rasha and her pogo stick, responds in an entirely unreasonable way, one we hadn't anticipated and for which we have no counterpoint.

"That Arab girl we see every day in the playground has one," she says. "Why don't you ask her if you can try it out?"

"That's a great idea," my father says. "You really should try it out before we buy it for you. Pogo sticks are not cheap, you know. What if you hate it? What if you're scared to jump? Just go up to her and ask if you can try it."

My brother and I exchange incredulous looks. Our parents don't get it. Rasha is older than us and intimidatingly pretty, with light skin and dark blond hair. She's Lebanese and only speaks Arabic on the playground, though we've heard her speak English a few times in a lilting French accent. She's usually surrounded by an impenetrable group of Arab kids, who are always laughing and talk-

ing loudly among themselves as they play with their new
gadgets. Even though Rasha seems quiet and kind, she is
entirely unapproachable—not just because she's cool, but
also because we're brown.

It's not like anyone has explicitly told my brother and
me about the hierarchies in this rich Arab country that we
moved to four years ago, where my father got a job making
almost double the money that he made back home. No one
has sat us down to talk about race, but we feel the hierarchies in our bones. We feel them in the fancy walled-off
compounds we get to visit sometimes where my father's
white European and American colleagues live, compounds
with swimming pools and gyms and armed police. We feel
them in the way my father is talked down to by Arab security guards, shopkeepers, restaurant hosts. We feel it in the
differences between the neighbors who say salaam to my
mother and those who don't, in the people who befriend
us—like Asma Aunty, who is also brown—and those who
don't. In this country, our brown skin makes us invisible,
like jinn. And so on the playground, my brother and I try not
to draw attention to ourselves. We play quietly with each
other in a corner of the park and entertain ourselves with
elaborate two-kid games. The other children never talk to
us, don't even seem to notice that we exist.

My mother, however, is undeterred by these unspoken
racial hierarchies that my brother and I notice—or maybe
she's sick of them, who knows? The day after listening to us
make our case for this pogo stick, she marches us over to
Rasha. We follow, embarrassed, trying to look anywhere but
at our mother—who is surprisingly nice, surprisingly charm-

ing when she asks Rasha if we can try out her pogo stick. "Sure!" says Rasha. "Not a problem at all!"

Our mother grins at my brother and me and goes back to her bench to read. We are shocked. And excited, too, but mostly shocked, too shocked even to be nervous, and entirely disbelieving of our good luck. We get on the pogo stick and try a few unsuccessful jumps; it's definitely harder than it looks and we fall down a lot on those first tries. Rasha's brother comes over to watch us struggle.

"If you break it, you have to pay us," he says.

Rasha is kinder. "Shut up, himar," she says to her brother, and pushes him away. She teaches us how to stand on the stick, how to hold on to the handles properly, how to dismount if we lose our balance, how to jump so it's not scary. It takes us awhile, but we get the hang of it. I even jump five times in a row before it's time for Maghrib prayer and we have to go home.

The next day on the playground we're less shy. Rasha waves to my brother and me; we go up to her and ask if we can play with her, have a turn with the pogo stick. She is patient with us. She shows us how to jump again and cheers us on when we do well. The three of us decide to make an obstacle course for her to navigate, with rocks and trash cans and anything else we can find. It is so fun that the Arab kids come and join us. One of the kids, who has a brand-new pink Casio Baby-G watch that her father bought her in England, times us all to see how long everyone can jump without falling. Rasha wins easily by minutes but cheers loudly and generously for the kid who comes in second place.

We're all having so much fun that no one notices when Rasha's parents drive up to the playground to pick her up. Usually Rasha and her brother pack up their things and run immediately to the car, but they're distracted today and their mother, who is blond and harshly beautiful, has to get out of the car. She spots us all playing together and walks over with a frown so deep it stuns my brother and me into pausing midplay. The other kids have seen her coming; they've all stopped playing and drifted away, and the only kids who are left in the circle are Rasha and her brother, and my brother and me.

Rasha's mother doesn't even look at us. She yells at her children in angry Arabic, grabs the pogo stick out of my brother's hands, and stomps back to the car.

"Bye," Rasha says to us hurriedly as she runs after her mother. "See you tomorrow."

But Rasha and her brother aren't at the playground the next day. None of the other Arab kids talk to us, even when we wave and try to say hi to the kids we had played with just the day before. *Are we invisible?* I wonder, and that makes me think of Asma Aunty's story. *Are my brother and I jinn? Are we able to appear and disappear?* I shudder and say *audhubillah,* asking Allah to protect me, like my mother has taught me to do when I'm scared. I don't share my suspicions with my brother, too afraid to voice the thought. Reluctantly, we go back to our corner of the park and play with each other.

The next day, Rasha is back, but she studiously ignores us, spends most of the time in the part of the playground where the much older kids hang out, and talks for a long time with an older girl in pink overalls. Toward the end of the evening, when she finally gets on her pogo stick, my brother has reached the limit of his patience and wants to go ask her if we can play. I try to talk him out of it. There's something weird going on, and I can sense it even if I can't name it, but my brother has the same streak of undeterred stubbornness as my mother. He walks right up to Rasha, me dragging my feet behind him. He taps her shoulder, even though a few of the meaner kids are around, even though Rasha's brother is right there, pretending to run everyone over with his bike.

"Hi, Rasha! Can we play with you?" my brother says.

"I'm so sorry. Not today!"

"Why not?" he says, even though I'm motioning at him to stop, even though I'm close to grabbing him and pulling him away.

"I don't think we can play together anymore. I'm really sorry. I had a lot of fun the other day, though," Rasha says kindly.

"But why?"

Rasha's brother answers this time. He bikes up to us and holds his nose. "Because our mom told us not to, stupid. It's because you're curry people. You smell nasty and you sound nasty and you're dirty. Stop making trouble for us. If we play with you, we'll become like you. Our clothes will smell like you. Our toys will smell like you. And we'll start to sound like you, with your stupid accents. Look at your skin, that dirt never washes off. Stop following us around. Go away before I make you go away."

We go away, back to our corner of the playground, back to being invisible.

III.

In seventh-grade biology, during a class on photosynthesis, our teacher pauses to ask if there are any questions.

"Miss! I have one," one of the popular girls asks from the back of the room. "Why do you wear hijab when this is a girls' school? There are no men around."

The class breaks into nervous giggles, like they do anytime one of the popular girls say anything to the teachers. I squirm in my seat near the front of the room, feeling awkward on our biology teacher's behalf, but also curious to hear what she'll say. My mother wears hijab and always seems relieved to be in the company of women so she can take it off.

"Well, I was hoping for questions about the reading or your homework . . ."

"Please, miss. I'm just curious. I've never met anyone who covers their hair from women."

"Okay, fine, I'll answer your question, but I don't want to repeat this again so listen well," my biology teacher says, taking a deep breath. "It's not women that I cover my hair from, it's jinn."

My palms start sweating. I know what's coming: a jinn story. My least favorite kind of story, ever since that night with Asma Aunty. I've learned to dodge these stories by stepping out of the room whenever someone is telling one, by begging friends to talk about something else. But I can't run away this time, it's too late to even ask to go to the bathroom.

"After some detailed study of the Quran and hadith, I've come to the decision that I should cover my hair from jinn. Let me tell you why: a few years ago, my cousin was at home alone and she went to the bathroom. Out of nowhere, a jinn appeared. My cousin wanted to take a shower so she wasn't wearing any clothes. She screamed, but the jinn wouldn't go away and kept coming closer and closer until it was inside her. It possessed her, girls."

My teacher pauses. The class is quieter, rapt with attention in a way it has never been before. I, on the other hand, have goosebumps all over my body. I look down at my biology textbook and attempt to read, trying to tune out my teacher's voice. Instead, I start to feel like I'm floating above the classroom, flying like a jinn and listening to this story from a distance, terrified and numb.

"What happened next, miss?" the popular girl says. Everyone collectively holds their breath.

"For days and days my cousin wasn't herself, kept bumbling words and saying all sorts of crazy things, but it wasn't her, it was the jinn speaking through her. Eventually, her family figured out what was going on and took her to a man who knew how to drive the jinn out of her body. This man said that the jinn possessed her because her head had been uncovered; the jinn was able to enter through her hair. Ever since then, I've been convinced that it's important for me to wear hijab all the time, even when we're not around men. You never know when jinn might desire you and want to possess you, so it's better to be able to cover yourself for protection. Okay, now that you've all heard the story, let's get back to the lesson. Can someone volunteer to read the practice problems? From the top of page thirty-two, please."

I'm so terrified that it takes me hours to come back into my body.

IV.

The year that I'm fifteen, I find myself groaning alongside the rest of the class when our tenth-grade math teacher tells us that we can't choose our own partners for our end-of-year project. She tells us she's decided who we're going to work with and that's that. The cries of "But why, miss" and "That's so unfair" start from the corner of the room where all the popular kids sit, and spread out until we're all whining. We're loud enough that the angry face of a passing school administrator pops into the hallway window and then we quiet down.

She's new, this math teacher, and generally well liked, which makes this authoritarian situation even more disappointing. As she passes out the assignment sheets for the project—mathematical calculations for designing a restaurant—it becomes clear that there's an added element of social engineering to her pairings: each group consists of two kids from different ends of the popularity spectrum who would otherwise never be friends with each other. It's an eye-roll-inducing rookie move—and my class doesn't hold back in telling her this.

"Miss, did you really pair up the nerds and the cool kids?"

"This isn't some high school movie, miss."

"This is so unfair! We're not magically going to become friends just because we work together."

I brace myself for whichever mean, popular kid I'm going to end up paired with. After my brief foray into coolness for pranking my beautiful and mysterious economics teacher who left at the end of last year, I'm back where I belong: at the front of the class with the other nerds. Lina, who I'm assigned to work with, doesn't even know my name. I know this for a fact, because when the teacher calls out our pair, Lina says, "Who?" and the whole class snickers. She looks at me like she's never seen me before, like I'm a jinn who has just materialized before her, even though we've been in classes together for years.

The lines of friendship are stark in my Islamic girls' international school that has kids from all over the world, and the hierarchies mirror those found in this country. Here, where two-thirds of the workforce is foreign, race is explicitly class: white Americans and Europeans are paid the most and hold the most prestigious jobs, followed by light-skinned Arabs in middle management, with South Asians holding mostly office and menial labor jobs. Nowhere are the consequences of this policy more apparent than in my high school, where the popular kids are all rich and fair-skinned, with straight hair and impeccable accent-free English from their summers abroad. Because it's an Islamic school, there are very few white kids, and the only other light-skinned girls at the top of the hierarchy are Arab. Lina fits all the criteria that put her at the top of the popularity pyramid, and I fit none. I'm as invisible to her as I was to Rasha and her pogo stick.

In class time that's dedicated to working on the project, Lina mostly ignores me, preferring to hang out and chat with her Arab friends. We exchange phone numbers and set up times to calculate how many liters of paint we'll need for our imaginary restaurant, but when Lina calls, she only wants the answers to our chemistry homework. She is the one who suggests meeting up at a coffee shop at the mall to work on the project, but spends the entire time flirting with the boys at the table next to us. Eventually I give up on her and do most of the work myself. Two days before it's due, I invite Lina over to my house to review our project, to do a final round of checking calculations, and to complete the cover art she's been drawing. She asks what neighborhood I live in, the nationalities of the people who live in my building, who else lives in my house, and says she'll ask her father. The next day, she says she can't come.

"Sorry, babe. My father is so overprotective," she says. "He said no because he was getting bad vibes about your place. He's the worst."

I swallow my feelings. *I shouldn't have asked in the first place, what a stupid idea,* I tell myself. What I say to Lina is "That's cool, no prob."

I'm relieved when we submit the project and our forced association is over, but the phone calls from Lina don't stop. She ends up calling me most nights for help with chemistry homework, and between balancing equations and calculating molarities, she fills me in on class gossip and tells me all about her life: the boy she's kind of sort of dating; the ugly, violent fistfights her brother gets into with her and their siblings; how scared she gets when her father yells at her mother. And because she tells me all about her life, I end up telling her about mine, too: how I can't wait to be done with high school, how I used to want to disappear.

My mother, sometimes a soothsayer and sometimes cruel, tells me one day after I get off a long, rambling phone call that Lina is using me. That I don't need to give her the answers to all the homework, don't need to spend hours on the phone explaining lessons and doing the job that my teachers are paid to do.

"You don't understand," I tell my mother. "Lina is my friend." I startle a little when I say it, unsure if it's true, unsure when I started believing that.

My mother is unconvinced. "People like that aren't friends with people like us," she says, and that makes me angry, one of my primary feelings that year. Hasn't she always taught us that everyone is the same in the eyes of God, that everyone—rich or poor, light-skinned or dark-skinned—is equal? Lina is just like us: sometimes funny, sometimes kind. Sometimes worldly, always impressionable. I hear her parroting a lot of what people around her say, but the upshot of this is that now she sometimes parrots me. I like spending time with Lina. I hope that we're friends.

My other friends at school are also skeptical when I start saying that Lina is my friend. But what else explains how often Lina hangs out with me between classes, how often she'll sit with me during lunch? Why else does she introduce me to her popular Arab friends, who begin to allow me into their circle? They teach me how to say the Arabic letter 'ayn properly, and Lina practices with me until I'm saying it right—so I sound like I'm speaking Arabic, she tells me, not some brown-people language. (It's Urdu, the name of the language is Urdu, I tell her a few times, but she can never remember, so I give up.) My new friends teach me curses and filler words in Arabic to pepper my speech with, like tuz and ya'ni, and using them makes me feel cool for the first time in my life.

One afternoon, they invite me to go with them to an expensive American burger place after school, a place that I've only been to once before with my parents as a post-exam treat. I don't have a ride to the restaurant because I'm the only one who goes home in the school bus instead of a chauffeured car, but Lina insists on me coming with her in her car. I bring all my Eid money to pay for the meal, but Lina pays for us both with a big banknote because she doesn't want to carry change. Afterward, she goes to her friend's house but has her driver drop me home. He's a sweet Pakistani man who asks me to call him Uncle Masood, who wants to know where my family is from and insists on meeting my father to say salaam. What explanation is there for all of this kindness from Lina, other than us being friends?

After summer break, two months of not seeing or talking to each other because she's been out of the country, Lina invites me and a couple of our classmates over to hang out at her place. It's my first time ever at an Arab friend's house. Uncle Masood picks me up and, on the drive over, makes small talk about how my family is doing and insists on sharing the steaming hot jalebi he just bought from the Indian neighborhood. When we get to Lina's place, he parks and motions me toward an ornate door. *No one is allowed in besides the family, guests, and maids,* Uncle Masood tells me before disappearing down a dingy corridor leading to the side room where he lives.

I ring the doorbell, a little scared of what to expect, a little scared that the summer apart will have changed our friendship. But Lina opens the door, screams in excitement when she sees me, and my anxieties melt. She ushers me inside. The ornate door leads into a residence complex where all of Lina's father's siblings and their families live, in huge houses enclosed within a boundary wall. Everything is bigger than I anticipated: the cars parked in the driveway, the swimming pool, the houses themselves. Lina's front hall is cavernous and casually opulent, with crystal chandeliers and gold brocade everywhere I look. I am too disoriented to notice how quiet it is, how empty of people. But not too dazzled to feel shame, to feel relieved that she never ended up coming to the cramped apartment I live in.

Lina leads me through several labyrinthine corridors to her bedroom. The room, too, is bigger than I anticipated, almost the size of my family's entire apartment. It's decorated in purple—her favorite color—and there is a TV and a computer and a phone, all in her bedroom. It's my dream room. I swallow the urge to say that, will myself to play it cool in front of the two friends who are here already—Lina's friends, really—two light-skinned Arab girls I'd gotten to know at the end of last school year. Lina has hooked up her digital camera to the TV, and they are all in the middle of looking at photos from her recent trip to Los Angeles. I join them in oohing and aahing over photos she's taken of the Sunset Strip, the beaches, and Lina's current animal obsession: golden retrievers. After a lot of badly framed photos of landscapes and dogs, we finally get to one of her with her family, posing in front of the Hollywood sign. I'm so curious about what they look like—the father she complains about so much, the mother she fights with, the fashionable and cool older siblings. It's kind of cute: they all look a lot like Lina and they're all in corny matching T-shirts and shorts.

"Oh! You're in shorts!" I say before I can stop myself from blurting out this very uncool thing to say.

Lina and her two friends look at each other and burst into laughter.

"Yeah?" Lina says. "What's wrong with shorts?"

"Nothing. I was just surprised. Your mom lets you wear shorts? And she wears shorts, too?"

I know I'm betraying myself, but this wearing of shorts is unimaginable to me, having spent the last eleven years of my life in this Arab country that has a public dress code. And they're all already laughing at me, so I figure why not satisfy my curiosity? My mother would never let me wear shorts, not inside the house, definitely not outside the house, and invokes the shaytan even when I wear short-sleeved shirts. And I know that no one in Lina's family is super religious, but my fifteen-year-old self who just started wearing hijab a few months ago—not because of modesty or needing to cover myself but to feel closer to Maryam, to feel closer to God—is still surprised at the legs on display.

"Well, yeah. It's so different over there. My mom says there aren't any creeps around, no dirty weirdos from all these backward countries like we have here. No one stares at you there, the way men do here. My mom says when we're in the U.S. we can wear whatever we want."

"But it's not like your mom has ever told you to wear hijab or cover up here, has she?" Lina's other friend asks.

"Just when we're outside the complex or in front of servants, you know, these people who you never notice but who are always around. Like our driver, Masood. You've all seen him, haven't you? With his dark mustache and beady eyes? He kinda looks like a rapist."

She's rolling her eyes when she's saying this but stops to look right at me when she continues.

"You know, we don't even allow him into the housing complex. He comes from a poor village, and you can tell he's never seen women like us before. He's the kind of person my mother tells me to cover from, so he's not tempted by me. It's so weird, wallah, you don't even notice him, but somehow he's always around, like a jinn. My mom says we should protect ourselves; it's better to be safe than to be sorry. You never know when someone like that might desire you. You know what I'm talking about, right, Lamya? You know what I mean by people like that? People who have never seen women like us? People who are kind of rapey?"

There's no malice in her voice; she's just trying to invite me into her world, onto her side. I swallow the big lump of anger that's rising in my throat and say something like yeah, yeah I guess so. I quickly change the topic and ask about all the clothes Lina bought in L.A. so I can tune out as I wonder what she means by covering to protect herself; it's not like people who wear hijab are magically protected from men. *And what does she mean by "people like that"? Does she mean brown people? Why would she need to protect herself from Uncle Masood and not the other men in her life? Is Uncle Masood a jinn? My dad has a dark mustache and beady eyes, is he scary, too? Do I look scary? Am I a jinn?* But then I get too nervous at these thoughts and tune back in, to Lina talking about all her favorite malls and stores in the U.S.—a different kind of torture.

V.

All week my brother and I have been dragged to various Eid parties, where our parents socialize with the few other brown families living in this large metropolitan city in this Arab country where none of us were born. It's so unfair. I'm six-teen and shouldn't have to go to these parties where we only see the same four other teens. We've become friends of sorts over years of forced socialization, but by the end of this week of parties, we're bored of each other. We're tired of eating biryani, playing endless games of cricket in our Eid clothes, and telling and retelling the same stories from school. *This party will be different,* my mother had promised me and my brother. *This one is at a rec center in a compound, and there'll be a game room where the kids can hang out. It has a pool table, foosball, Ping-Pong, even.* But when we get to the party, the pool set is missing half the balls, the foosball table has broken men, and curiously, there's no Ping-Pong table, just paddles and a ball. The six of us end up in the exact situation we wanted to avoid: being bored.

We're sitting around the entirely unusable game room when Majid, who is seventeen and the oldest among us, announces that we should tell jinn stories. I glance at my brother. Neither of us has forgotten the terror we felt hearing Asma Aunty's story all those years ago, but of the two of us, I'm the one who hates jinn stories more, who still sometimes has nightmares. I consider protesting, but hesitate, not wanting to admit my fear. I look to my brother for backup, but he stares forward resolutely, refusing to make eye contact with me.

"Last chance for any scaredy-cats to go hold hands with their mommies," Majid taunts, motioning toward the door, and just like that, I'm stuck.

"Someone shut the door and turn off the light," another friend says gleefully. My stomach churns and my pits start sweating. This friend loves Halloween and spooky things, and she looks like she's about to launch into a story when she's cut off by Majid.

"I get to start because it was my idea," he says. "I have a really good one. So this is real, everyone. My aunt told me this story and she swore to God, she said wallahi it was true . . ."

I close my eyes so I can pretend that the lights are on, start mentally reciting Ayat al-Kursi. My maulvi saab—the imam at the nearby mosque who used to teach my brother and me Quran—had told us to read this verse to invoke Allah's protection.

"This happened to my aunt's best friend's mom's sister, Nasreen," Majid begins. "This one time, Nasreen was sitting in the mosque, doing duaa and tasbeeh. This woman comes up to her, shuffling from side to side like she's having trouble walking. The woman is in an abaya and full niqab, covered from head to toe. She's wearing gloves and socks; no part of her body is visible. The whole thing is weird because it's in the women's section of the mosque and this woman didn't need to be so covered, you know?"

Majid drops his voice, and everyone leans in to listen. I, on the other hand, lean decidedly out. *Allahu la illah illa huwal hayyul gayyum*, I say to myself, repeating the first line of the verse over and over.

"So this woman comes up to Nasreen and says that something is wrong, says she needs help right away. She asks Nasreen to come with her to the women's bathroom in the basement. Nasreen is terrified. She doesn't know this woman and she doesn't want to go anywhere with her. Luckily, Nasreen doesn't buy it and says to her, 'I've never seen you here at the mosque before. What's your name? What do you do?' The woman doesn't answer, so Nasreen asks again. 'Who are you? Show me your face! Show me who you are!' But instead of answering the questions, the woman disappears."

There's a gasp that I recognize in the dark as my brother's. My friend who loves spooky things lets out a delighted scream.

"Poof. Just like that. The only things left behind are her

abaya and gloves and socks. Her clothes fall to the ground, entirely empty. Nasreen starts screaming and has been too freaked out to leave the house since. Okay, I'm done. No, we can't turn the lights on yet. Stop being babies. Let's have another story. Who wants to go next?"

VI.

When I am seventeen, I move for the second time in my life—but this time, all on my own. I move away from all the people I know in the Arab country I've grown up in, even farther away from the country I was born in, across the ocean, to the United States.

My uncle, whom I haven't seen in almost a decade, is tasked with picking me up from the airport, settling me into the prestigious college I've scored a scholarship at, and teaching me how to live in yet another new country. My uncle moved here twenty years ago for college not knowing anyone, so he takes this job seriously: at the arrivals gate he hugs me and hands me a bag of Doritos. It's my first lesson in blending in, he says, because Americans love snacks.

My uncle now has a house in the suburbs of a city that's a few hours' drive away from the college I'll be attending. I spend a week at his place before he drops me off at the campus, and it's a real culture shock to be in the suburbs in the middle of nowhere, after the cosmopolitan city I grew up in with people from all over the world. Here everyone looks the same and dresses the same and does the same things. "Is this what Americans are like?" I ask my uncle after a trip to Costco. That night, he and his wife make me watch *Friends* so I can learn the answer.

The next day, while I'm doing a crossword on the couch, my uncle's lessons continue.

"What do you call that thing you're chewing?" he asks. The thing I'm chewing very ungracefully is the pink end of my pencil.

"Um. A rubber?"

He shrieks. "No! You can't say that. It's called an eraser. Rubber means something very different here."

"Okay, okay!" I say. "Lesson learned."

The day after, we're picking out bedding for my dorm room when he asks me what race Will Smith is.

"I don't know," I say, worried about misstepping.

"He's African American, okay? You can't use any other words you'll hear."

I nod solemnly.

Later, my uncle takes me to his office. It's a Sunday evening; no one else is there and the photocopier is free. He makes me a double-sided copy of my passport and visa, then trims the page carefully with scissors so it'll fit into my wallet without bending.

"Whatever you do, don't go anywhere without this copy of your papers. And as soon as you get your student ID, do the same thing. You'll need those three things on you at all times."

I'm not sure I understand why he's telling me to do this,

but in those days, I do as I'm told. After we're done at the office, we pick up pizza on our way home. There's an American football game on, and my uncle has promised to teach me the rules.

My uncle's advice about carrying photocopies of my documents comes in handy. After the first week of college, once all the parents and siblings and stragglers leave campus, I end up being asked for my ID a lot. I take it in stride at first, happy to show off my shiny new student ID, happy to make small talk with security people. But then, halfway through the semester, a substitute teaching assistant asks to see my student ID when I walk into the room where we're having class. She says she needs to check the spelling of my name against the roster even though she doesn't check anyone else's name. I find it very odd.

After the incident with the TA, I realize that I get asked for my ID a lot more than other people. And there are clear patterns. I'm asked for my ID the most when I'm alone—crossing the quad to get to my dorm after a late meeting, working in the computer lab early one morning, in the sports center walking to soccer practice—and usually, it's under the guise of asking if I'm lost. It happens less when I'm with others—although once, a whole group of my Black and brown friends from the Muslim Student Association get asked for our IDs when we're trying to get access to a study room in the library, a building that we needed to swipe our IDs to get into in the first place. It *never* happens when I'm with a group of mostly white people, like my soccer teammates, with whom I'm able to saunter into a party in swanky upperclassmen housing without the security person even lifting up her head to look at us.

"You're being asked to show your ID because you look so young," my white teammate tells me.

"Obviously, it's because you wear hijab," says my friend from the MSA, who started wearing a headscarf two years ago, to whom everything is about hijab.

"Listen, I'm the only one who'll tell it like it is," says my one Republican friend, a white boy named Dave I met in my Intro to Physics class, one late night while we're doing a problem set together in the dining hall. "You're being asked for your ID because you're Muslim. We're fighting a war against Muslims right now, so they're all scary; we never know who will do what and when. We need to know who's around."

It feels like the truest answer I've gotten from anyone, and it's clear that my friend doesn't think I'm part of this "they" or "us." But I'm confused about where this leaves me—about how his response can somehow make me feel seen and unseen. Like a jinn.

"Right," I say to Dave. "Right."

As fall turns to winter, I begin to get the hang of deciphering the hierarchies of this country. I notice that my Black friends are treated horribly by everyone in authority; my friends with accents are assumed to be stupid; my immigrant friends are always being asked where they're really from. I notice that people who are white or appear to be white are on top of the pyramid here just like they were in the country where my parents and brother still live, that sometimes this category of "appears to be white" includes wealthy, worldly, light-skinned Arabs like Rasha and Lina, but not always. I notice that this category doesn't include Arabs who are visibly Muslim, who have identifiably Arab names. I learn that my brown hijabi Muslim body is seen as scary, disempowered, both hypervisible and invisible at the same time.

So I start pushing back when asked for my ID. That spring, a security guard approaches me while I'm parking my bike before a meeting with my academic adviser. Of course, he asks to see my ID.

For the first time, I don't immediately move to pull out my papers. "What for?" I ask.

He looks briefly startled by the question but recovers quickly. "It's just protocol. Look, I'm going to ask that man, too."

He makes a big show of walking over to a white man parking his fancy carbon-frame bicycle and looks directly at me while asking to see this man's ID.

"See? I ask everyone, not just you," he says when he saunters back. I slowly fish my ID out of my wallet, taking my time going through all the cards in there, even though I know exactly where it is. It feels like a small act of resistance to make him wait.

The next person I push back on is more apologetic. I'm finishing an experiment in a science lab. I'm at a bench, gloves on, in the middle of pipetting a small volume of DNA into a tube, when a security guard passes by the rest of my classmates, who are preparing to leave, and asks to see my ID.

"What? Why?" I ask.

"I'm so sorry," he says. "I know you, I've seen you in this building many times before, but I just have to confirm for my supervisor. We were told that there was a security breach in this building by someone in a red T-shirt."

I'm definitely wearing a T-shirt. But it is light gray.

And then I graduate college, move to New York, and go out into the real world. One Saturday morning, I'm riding a Greyhound bus to visit my uncle and his family upstate when we get stopped randomly for a spot check. It has been a quiet morning and an uneventful ride, with most people dozing as the bus rocks us to sleep. But suddenly the bus pulls over to the side of the road and a uniformed man with a gun and a Taser gets on. We all wake up, sit upright and alert. The man lumbers through the aisles, looking at all of our faces, and stops right in front of me. He asks to see the IDs of two people on the bus that day: first me—the only visibly brown, visibly Muslim person on the bus—and then a white woman sitting a few rows down, the usual decoy. Luckily, I've brought my passport and my visa stamp is unexpired. Luckily, I don't need extra paperwork to prove the legality of my being in the country—extra paperwork that, thanks to my uncle's advice, I always carry photocopies of wherever I go. After countless encounters, I've learned how to talk to uniformed men with guns: lots of yes sirs, no sirs, calm breathing, and feigned nonchalance. He flips through my mostly empty foreign pass-port, hands it back, and moves on. We are able to continue to our destination a few minutes later.

Luckily, I've learned enough to know when not to push back.

VII.

My first year of graduate school in New York I'm hanging out with a friend from the mosque, Rashid, who is starting a grad program that fall. We're drinking bubble tea at a park, waiting for his wife, Salwa, to join us after she's done with work. It's a rare day where I don't have very much going on, no deadlines to worry about, no meetings, and I'm grateful for our leisurely evening together. But of course, I spend it complaining about my department and how stupid I feel compared to all the white people in my program.

"It's so annoying how well they do," I whine to Rashid. "I get higher grades, but somehow they're best friends with all the professors? They keep winning all these awards and landing the best internships. They're just so much better than me."

"Yeah, I've never had that problem," Rashid says, slurp-ing a bubble.

"You've never had white people in your classes?" I ask.

"No, that whole being intimidated by white people thing. That thing you just did where you assumed white people were better than you."

I'm about to protest when it comes to me. I do assume that white people are better than me. It's hard not to after years of being the brown person asked to show their ID. All the times it felt like white people literally couldn't see me: when they'd cut ahead of me in line, forget to distribute handouts to me in class, give instructions to people behind me even though I was right in front of them. Or the times when I felt like an exhibit: when white people would stare at me as I walked by, not sit next to me on the bus when I was talking to my parents in Urdu, pull their children away. And further back, too: Lina getting bad vibes about coming to my house, Rasha and her pogo stick, the people I grew up around who would and wouldn't say salaam to my parents. It's no wonder that I feel like a jinn, seen and unseen. It's no wonder that I think they're better than me.

"How have you gotten away with not internalizing this?" I ask Rashid after a pause. "You grew up Black in the U.S.!"

"Yeah, but my parents were Garveyites," he says. "They never instilled in us this idea that white people were superior to us. We grew up with stories about Malcolm X and the Black Panthers. If anything, I grew up feeling sorry for white people. But not too sorry."

"That's so unfair! I grew up with my family reminiscing fondly about being colonized by the British!"

Rashid laughs so hard that bubble tea comes out of his nose. As he's sitting there, wiping a mixture of snot and purple-colored liquid off his face, I decide it's okay for me to admit to something embarrassing.

"Listen, Rashid—you can't tell anyone this—but when I was younger, I used to wonder if being brown made me a jinn. Because sometimes it would feel like white people just couldn't see me, but also sometimes it was like I was this scary, disgusting creature. Even now I'm not fully convinced I'm not a jinn . . ."

Rashid listens more solemnly than I was anticipating. "Yeah, that's shit you have to unlearn," he says. "It's not your race that makes you feel like a jinn. It's white supremacy."

"What do you mean?" I ask, stunned.

"It's white supremacy that got in your head. It's white supremacy that makes people scared of you or not see you. And it's white supremacy that makes you internalize those things and makes you feel inferior to white people. That's shit you have to unlearn. You have to dispossess yourself of those false narratives."

But is it possible to be dispossessed, once the possession has already entered your body, wisped into your brain, sneaky as smoke, and settled somewhere in your bones? How do you undo a lifetime of experiencing racism, of whispers and warnings? Of these feelings that have been swirling inside you your whole life: fear, disgust, anxiety, revulsion—directed at yourself?

Rashid points me to resources: books by Audre Lorde and bell hooks and Angela Davis, all of which I devour. I go to lectures on postcolonial history and blaze with anger at the injustice. I go to a talk at the Islamic center about Malcolm X. Afterward, I read his autobiography, and from there, move on to reading about the Black Panthers, resistance movements, the legacies of slavery and settler colonialism in the United States. I read about the structural dimensions of racism—class differences, environmental racism, and

the racial demographics of prisons and policing. I read
Frantz Fanon and learn about decolonization struggles in
the world. I read Ngũgĩ wa Thiong'o and learn about decolo-
nizing one's mind.

Slowly, it starts to sink in that it's racism that's the problem, not race; that it's white supremacy that's the problem,
not me; it's white supremacy that needs to be fought and
dismantled.

VIII.

As for jinn: I'm on the subway back home from visiting a
friend in Brooklyn one day, reading the Quran in a near-
empty train. It's Ramadan and I'm trying to finish it in thirty
days, trying to read chapters while I'm waiting or unoccu-
pied, in the rare moments in between the busyness of this
month. I get to Surat al-Jinn.

Usually I avoid this surah: thinking about jinn makes
me feel so scared and disgusted that I switch from the English translation to reading the Arabic I can't understand. But
today feels different. Now that I've lived in the city for a few
years, I'm not scared or disgusted by much—not rats on the
train platform, not creaky apartment noises, not weird
smells on the street. And something about the train—the
bright lights and the movement, being alone but also among
other people doing their own thing—makes it less daunt-
ing to understand the meaning of Surat al-Jinn. This time, I
keep reading.

Say [O, Muhammad]: it has been revealed to me that
a group of jinn once listened in [on the Prophet] and
said, "We have heard a wondrous Quran
That gives guidance to the right path, and we have
come to believe it. We shall never associate partners
with our Lord . . .
Some of us are righteous and others less so: we follow
different paths . . .
And when we heard the [Quran], we came to believe
in it: whoever believes in his Lord need fear no loss
nor injustice.
Some of us submit to [God] and others go the wrong
way: those who submit to God have found wise
guidance . . ."
Say: I have no control over any harm or good that may
befall you. (72:1–21)

I read these verses and find myself shaking—not with
fear this time but with clarity and adrenaline. I've been
wrong this whole time. They're just like us, jinn. They're not
creatures who are out to get us, not creatures we need to
wear hijab around, not creatures we need to fear. Some are
righteous, some less so. Some believe in God, some don't.
Sometimes they listen in on us and sometimes they fly into
the heavens and sometimes they're mischievous. Like us,
but different.

I make myself take deep breaths. Now that I've been
reading about antiracism, I know that difference should not
mean scary, difference should not mean less than. Which

means that jinn are not dirty, not nasty, not something others need protection from, just like my brown skin doesn't
make me dirty or nasty or something others need protection
from. My brown skin and my hijab don't make me less than,
don't make white people and light-skinned Arabs better
than me. *Now I know,* I tell myself. *Now I need to stop hating
jinn. And then I can stop hating myself.*

ALLAH

I.

In the beginning, there was a God. (But is it the beginning if it always was?)

Before the beginning, there was a God. A God named Allah: *Al* as in "the," *lah* as in "God," the God, *Allah*—the God who always was.

In the beginning, God created the world, and then after that, God created the word: names for everything, everything in the world.

———

As part of the beginning, God taught us these words. Taught us language, and with it, names for each other, for creatures, for feelings and concepts and everything in between.

And using this language, God taught us about God. Ninety-nine names so lush, layered, and specific, so that we may know our Creator, our God. *Al-Rahman,* the Most Merciful. *Al-Hakam,* the Arbitrator of Justice. *Al-Raoof,* the Most Kind. *Al-Fattah,* the Opener of Hearts and Destinies for Those Who Implore. *Al-Wadud,* the One Who Loves More Magnanimously and More Intensely Than a Mother. *Al-Ghafoor,* the Forgiver; *Al-Ghaffar,* the Repeatedly Forgiving; *Al-Tawwaab,* the Acceptor of Forgiveness; *Al-Afuu',* the Eraser of Sins. Names that push the boundaries of our imagination. Names that teach us expansiveness.

II.

At six years old, I have a lot of questions about God, which my parents defer to my maulvi saab, who teaches my brother and me how to read the Quran. Every day, exactly thirty minutes after Asr prayer, my maulvi saab bikes to our apartment, his ankles flashing under his sunnah-cut shalwars, his curly black beard unruly, and his white kurta crisp and sweatless—no minor miracle in the midday sun. Sometimes my brother and I are outside playing when we see him flying down the road. When this happens, we hide from him: we run around the building and duck behind a hedge in hopes of having the day off from our lesson. But then our mom comes to the window and screams, *I know you're out there, you need to come inside NOW, if I have to come get you I'll hit you,* and we skulk back inside for our daily lesson.

It's not that we don't like our maulvi saab, we do. He smiles a lot and wears a different colored kufi every day. Never yells, never hits us, and is patient when we make mistakes, unlike some of the maulvi saabs we hear about from our friends. It's just that it's a drag to read from the Quran when we could be playing on the swing set in the nearby park or watching the older kids in our neighborhood play soccer. Instead, we have to sit at the dining table and read the Quran. I read two pages, and my brother, who is significantly slower than me at remembering letters, reads one page. Just the Arabic, just sounding out these words we don't understand from the Quran. Every day, thirty minutes after Asr prayer, with my maulvi saab.

After we're done—if we read well, don't take too long, and don't make too many mistakes—our maulvi saab tells us stories from the Quran. We hear stories of prophets and whales and arks, babies born of miracles, little boys left in wells by jealous brothers, little boys who grow up to be prophets. And we get to ask questions, whatever we want, even questions that make my mother say, *Tawbah, tawbah, from where did you get this question, ask Allah for forgiveness.* The sliver of time after I'm done reading my two pages, while we're waiting for my brother to finish, is when I decide one day to ask my maulvi saab a very important question that I haven't been able to stop thinking about.

"Is Allah a man?"

My brother, who is finishing off the end of his page, stops reading midverse to listen.

"My cousin said Allah is a man," I say. He's a few years older than me, this cousin, and is visiting us from a different city. He knows a lot of things, but lies a lot, too, and I don't know what to believe and I'm confused. In my mind, Allah has always been a woman, floating and ethereal in the night sky, wrapped in white dupattas and with a face like the moon, a face that looks suspiciously like my grandmother's. To think of Allah as a man has been destabilizing.

"Your cousin is wrong, Allah is not a man," my maulvi saab says.

"Is Allah a woman?" my brother asks incredulously, all pretense at reading dropped.

"No, Allah is not a woman, either."

"But then how come we say Allah mian?" I demand. This Urdu word for sir is what my cousin has used as evidence for Allah being a man, and it's been eating away at me since.

"Mian is just a term of respect, like you would use for an elder uncle. That doesn't mean anything. Allah is not a man or a woman. Allah is Allah. Hurry up and finish reading so I can tell you the rest of the story of Prophet Yusuf."

My brother cheers and goes back to reading. I do want to know the rest of the story of Prophet Yusuf, so I give it up. But lying in bed later that night, I have more questions. How come no one says Allah baji or Allah aapa? Those are terms of respect, too, but I've only heard them used for women. Allah ends with -ah like the names of most of the girls I know, so how come Allah isn't a woman? How can Allah not be a man or a woman? What else is there? And even though I can't quite put this into words at six years old, the outlines of a question begin to appear inside me: Is it possible that I, too, might be this something else?

That night, I say my duaas in bed imagining Allah the same as I always have, floating and ethereal like a moon, just without the dupattas. Allah's face still looks like my grandmother's.

III.

When I'm ten, my brother and I start going to a version of Islamic Sunday school. It's not exactly Sunday school—it's on Wednesday evenings, for one, and it's not organized by a mosque, it's organized by my mom's new friend and some other aunties and uncles. It's supposed to make Islam exciting and fun for kids, and for the most part, it does: two short lessons, with the second one always being some sort of game or skit or coloring activity. There's a snack break between the lessons, with an array of chips and chocolates and other junk food that my mother is stingy about at home, with extra candy for kids who have done their homework. Afterward, we play long games of cricket or soccer or freeze tag while we're waiting for our parents to pick us up.

I look forward to Wednesdays all week. Unlike most of the other kids at our Sunday school, I'm diligent about doing homework, I'm good at memorizing facts, and I'm especially good at following rules. One week, the lesson is on how to

do wudu before praying, and I master it easily, even demon-
strating my feet-wiping technique for the class the week
after. The next week's lesson is on how to pray and I crush
it, memorizing all the duaas and then training myself to pray
five times a day. The aunties and uncles who teach the
classes love me; they're always showering me with candies
and compliments. And then I get to play sports and hang
out with my friends afterward. Wednesdays are my favorite
day of the week.

A few months in, the aunty who runs the intermediate
level class tells my mom that I'm ready to move up. I have
the basics down, she says, and it's time I move to the advanced class. This advanced class is taught by Uncle Karim,
who is a rock star. Or so I hear from my friend who's two
years older than me and in his class. I hear that Uncle Karim
jokes about video games and pop stars, that he hands out
Jolly Ranchers and makes everyone laugh. I'm ecstatic and
also a little intimidated: the class is full of teenagers who are
older and taller than me. I don't really know any of them,
and what if I don't understand the lesson, what if I ask stupid questions? But the first class I attend goes well. We're
reading the translation of Surat al-Nahl, the chapter of the
bee, and it's full of sumptuous descriptions of nature. Uncle
Karim is welcoming and funny, makes us all giggle when
he reminds us to pray fi-sabillillah, for the sake of Allah, not
fi-sabilil-aunty, for the sake of the aunties who might be
watching.

The second class is even more exciting. We're reading
the translation of Ayat al-Kursi, the verse of the throne,
which describes Allah. My grandma taught me this ayah in

Arabic when I was five and I have been reciting it since—
every morning when I wake up, every night with my mother
when she tucks me into bed, every time I wake up in the
middle of the night and it's dark and I'm scared. I read the
ayah before every exam at school and every time I get on an
airplane, and I'm excited to finally find out what it means.
Uncle Karim hands out photocopies of the English translation; we read the meaning aloud together and I'm mesmerized by the descriptions of God. *Al-Hayy,* the One Who Has
Always Been Living. Neither sleep nor tiredness touches
Him. His is whatever is in the heavens and the earth. He
knows what comes before and after each moment in the life
of man. Nothing escapes His knowledge. His throne is as
vast as the universe. And He is the *Al-Aliy,* the Most High,
Al-Adhim, the Most Magnificent.

We're all in awe, quieter than usual and hanging on to
every word that Uncle Karim is saying. It takes us all class
to get through this one verse; he dissects it one characteris-
tic of God at a time, and we're enthralled. But there's one
thing that's been bothering me and just before class ends, I
raise my hand.

"I have a question," I say shyly. "How come the translation says he? Isn't Allah not supposed to be a man or a
woman?"

Uncle Karim pauses for a second and looks thoughtful
before he answers me.

"It's just translating the Arabic word huwa, which means
he in English. It's just convention, Lamya—that means it's
the traditional way of translating the word. It doesn't mean
that God is a man."

This doesn't feel like explanation enough. "But then why doesn't the Quran say the Arabic word for she?"

"It's like when people say postman or fireman, but they mean both men and women."

"But that's not fair, either."

"It's just convention, Lamya. There's just no other way to say it. Because of the conventions of language at that time and even now, Allah had to say *he* instead of *she*. Saying *she* would have been weak sauce."

The class giggles and Uncle Karim moves on. But I'm indignant, silently seething with even more questions. Did Uncle Karim just say that women are weak? Did Allah say that women are weak? If Allah is all powerful, couldn't Allah change language and convention? This doesn't sit right with me, but by now I know that these are not questions I'm going to find the answers to from Uncle Karim, from Islamic Sunday school—perhaps not from anyone other than myself.

IV.

I'm twenty-three years old and still newish to living in New York, still finding my footing in this city and looking for my people, my Muslim community. A friend of a friend invites me to a halaqa study circle that she started with some college friends who were interested in creating a Muslim feminist space, and I start going. The women at this halaqa are all a few years older than me, all first-generation immigrants with professional degrees, corporate jobs, and husbands, all just starting to have babies. We don't have a ton in common, but I love having a space that centers spiritual growth, I love that we can discuss complicated Muslim things: the long article that just came out on women who stopped wearing hijab, or the latent xenophobia of progressive Muslim groups in the city.

This month in the halaqa, we're making our way through a Sufi treatise on spirituality, reading a few chapters at a time and discussing how the principles therein are relevant to our lives. But one week, the discussion about cleansing one's heart of jealousy devolves into complaining about how hard it is to find good nannies, how expensive child care is. The next week, we get sidetracked into talking about where to buy dining chairs, another conversation in which I say almost nothing, having never bought a dining chair in my life. The more I keep going to this halaqa, the clearer it is that I don't fit in. I feel fourteen again—surrounded by people living lives that I don't want. I know I confuse these women by how much I seem like them—a brown, hijab-wearing graduate of an elite college—while adamantly turning down their efforts to set me up with a man. *I have Maryam,* I tell myself on subway rides back to my apartment after the halaqas. *I don't have to live like them.* But it feels lonelier in this context than it ever did before.

One week, the friend of a friend invites her cousin to the halaqa. The host of this week's meeting lives in a swanky building in midtown, and I find myself sitting on a decked-out rooftop in the shadow of tall luxury skyscrapers. It's just after Maghrib and the sun has dipped behind the buildings, leaving the sky cough-syrup pink in its wake. Above us rises the crown of the Chrysler Building, so close that it illuminates the books on our laps, so close that the gargoyles seem to be eavesdropping. It is so beautiful. Distracted by the view, I lose track of the conversation. When I tune back in, the friend's cousin is talking. She's my age and is visiting the city for a few days to find an apartment and sign a lease before she moves here for her new management consulting job. She seems edgier and less conformist than the other women at this halaqa, and I watch her closely, wondering if she might be someone I can befriend. She's talking right now about her relationship with someone who is a she, about building a connection through prayer and dhikr, and I'm intrigued until I realize with a start that she's not talking about a woman, she's talking about God. She's talking about God using *she* as a pronoun.

The other women must have been similarly jarred because one of them interrupts her.

"Wait, hold up, you're using *she* for God."

"Yeah," the cousin says, and I can tell by the smirk on her face that she's been looking forward to the moment when we'd catch on. "It's a thing I've decided to do. All the Islamic feminists have been writing about it. It's a really important way to fight the patriarchy."

"But Allah isn't a woman," I find myself saying in an angrier tone than I anticipated.

"Allah isn't a man, either," the cousin says.

"But using *she* is weird, too. It just reinforces the gender binary, no?" I look around to see if anyone agrees and am met with vacant stares.

"So what? Representation matters. That's what feminism is about. And there aren't any other alternatives anyway."

"Yes, there are. *It. Ze. They.*" One of the women takes out her phone and starts scrolling. Someone else gets up to go to the bathroom.

Meanwhile, the cousin is getting more and more worked up. "None of those work. *It* is so disrespectful to use for God. I don't even know what *ze* is. And, *astaghfirullah, they* is blasphemous; Allah isn't plural."

"But Allah uses the royal *we* in the Quran all the time! Why can't we use a royal *they*?"

"Because that's what the transgenders use."

"Yeah. Exactly. It's a good way to express gender nonconformity. If Allah isn't a man or a woman, maybe Allah is trans."

The cousin turns an indignant red. "*Audhubillah.* How can you say that?" But the anger in her tone is at least something, unlike the rest of the women in the group, who look bored—as if they can hear me but can't understand the words I'm saying, as if this groundbreaking realization that I'm having about God is not relevant to their lives. A few of them flip ahead in their books. Some even start talking to each other.

I'm about to reply to the cousin when the host steps in and asks a question, entirely unrelated to gender, about the next paragraph in the reading. The group coalesces again and the space fills with chatter. Within minutes, they've moved on from the reading and are entrenched in a conversation about meditation and how helpful yoga is for training your mind. This idea of Allah as trans feels erased from the

space, and maybe it's dramatic to feel this way, but it feels
as if the idea of transness itself has been erased from the
space. I'm jarred by how personally I'm taking this; it's not
me they're erasing from the space, but it feels that way. I
ask myself for the three thousandth time what the fuck I'm
doing here, with these women, on this swanky rooftop, in
this halaqa. That's the last time I go to the study circle.

I don't find my people, my Muslim community at that
halaqa. But I learn something else: how important it is for
me to use the pronoun *they* for God—my God, whom I refuse to define as a man or a woman, my God who tran-
scends gender. I learn that I can remove myself from
situations where people aren't interested in this conception
of God as genderqueer, of God as nonbinary, of God as
trans. And I learn that I want to explore what these gender-
expansive concepts mean for my own sense of self, too.

V.

In the beginning, God created a person. A person made out
of clay—not just any clay: black clay.

In the beginning, God created a person, a Black person, lovingly proportioned and shaped. God named this person Adam,
and then God breathed into Adam a soul. Made from this
soul her mate.

From *her*, from Adam, this first soul, her mate. *Khalaqa minha zawjaha*, Surat al-Nisa, the chapter of the women, in verse number one: "Oh humanity! Be mindful of your Lord Who created you from a single soul, and made from her, her mate." *Khalaqa*, meaning "created from," *minha*, meaning "from her," *zawjaha*, meaning "her mate."

And God created, too, this language, to teach us. This Arabic, the language of the Quran, in which all words are supposedly gendered. Adam, a name, a masculine word; *nafs*, soul, a feminine word. This person, Adam, the first person created, gendered as both masculine and feminine, created holding both, by a God who is neither. This Adam, from whom came her mate, Hawa.

This Adam and Hawa live blissfully in paradise, ignorant of their nakedness, ignorant of both gender and genitalia. Until, tempted by Satan, they eat from the forbidden tree and their bodies are revealed to them. They cover themselves and are exiled to earth, a place where, among the legacy of their punishments to all of their descendants, is the consciousness, the rigidity of gender.

VI.

I start my period when I'm eleven years old, and my mother tells me that I'm a woman now. Overnight, this becomes the refrain that defines all my experiences. I need to close my legs when I sit because I'm a woman now. I need to put effort into my appearance because I'm a woman now. I don't like wearing earrings but my mother buys me some at the mall because I'm a woman now. I can't play cricket with the boys in shalwar kameez and dupatta, which I had to wear to the dinner party because I'm a woman now. And I need new friends who aren't boys, and if I play nice with the girl who lives in the building next to us we'll go to the bookstore and I can buy one new paperback—all because I'm a woman now.

It's always been like this between my mother and me, this struggle over the kind of daughter she wishes she had and the one she ended up with: an irascible tomboy who can't stop getting into trouble. Her longing hits a peak the summer that I'm thirteen. My uncle—her brother—is getting married. We travel to the country I was born in for this wedding, this spectacular event that consists of five different parties stretched over eight days. Each party requires a different outfit. Each outfit has to be designed. Each design has to be tailored and tried on and readjusted, and then matched with bangles, shoes, and a purse. For my mother, this is thrilling: the deadlines and the racing around the city and the dyeing dupattas to match shalwars, all in the pursuit of beauty. For me, who has to accompany her on these errands because I'm a woman now, this is an exquisite form of torture.

I'm relieved when the day of the first party finally, finally arrives. All the outfits have been acquired, all that is left is the wearing of them and being careful not to spill food on them. That afternoon, I'm watching cricket in the TV room with my brood of cousins when my mother and her sister call me into the air-conditioned room where the women are getting ready. I'm not supposed to get dressed until half an hour before we leave because I can't be trusted not to wrinkle my shalwar kameez, and there are hours and hours to go until then, but my mother and her sister pull me into the room anyway. It's chaotic in here: blindingly bright lights and strong perfume and all the women in various states of undress, in various stages of makeup and pinning up of hair.

"We want to put some lipstick on you," my aunt says. "I have this new shade that will look gorgeous with your skin tone."

"No, thank you," I say. I need to get back to the cricket match; my favorite batsman is at the crease and I can hear my cousins cheering in the other room.

"Please? I promise you can take it off if you don't like it," my aunt says.

"No, thank you," I say again, firmer.

My aunt turns to my mother. "Uff, where did we go wrong with this one? Why is she such a problem child?"

"I promise you can take it off if you don't like it," my mother says. "Just try it?"

I take a second to calculate. If I try on the lipstick, I can say I don't like it and take it off immediately. The whole thing will take three minutes and then I can go back to watching cricket, instead of the half an hour of arguing and crying that it'll take to stand my ground.

"Okay, fine. Put the lipstick on. But can you do it quickly?"

My mother's face lights up with joy. My aunt sits me down in a chair before I can change my mind, positions me with my back to the mirror, and makes me close my eyes. Suddenly, they're both dabbing at my face.

"Wait, what are you doing? I thought you said lipstick?"

"We're just putting on a little bit of foundation. You can't really put on lipstick without foundation, it looks weird in photos. You won't even notice it's on, trust me."

I'm still figuring out how to respond to this when they start dabbing at my eyes.

"What are you doing to my eyes?"

"It's just a little eye shadow. You can't really wear lipstick and foundation without a little bit of eye shadow, and we're going to put on a tiny bit of eyeliner and mascara. Now keep your eyes closed, I don't want to poke you by mistake."

Suddenly I'm being prodded and drawn on and things are being rubbed into my face and it's so unfair because I definitely did not agree to this and I have no idea what's going on but I can't even open my eyes because of all the sharp objects in use.

After what feels like hours, my aunt spins my chair around so I'm facing the mirror and tells me to open my eyes.

"Look! You're so pretty now!"

But I have no idea who this person is that I'm looking at; it's not me. It's some other person with my face and I hate it: I hate how it feels, I hate how it looks. They've made me look three shades lighter than I usually am; they've made me look like a woman in ways that I don't feel. It's all so unfair and I hate it and I want to wash it off; they promised I could wash it off and I tell them that.

"Don't be ridiculous. You're glowing," my mother says.

"We put so much effort into doing your makeup! You can't just wash it off," says my aunt.

Some of my other aunts and great-aunts and cousins come by and tell me I look so grown up, that I look like a woman now. So beautiful, they tell me. So pyaari. Pretty. No one has called me that before.

I feel so confused and disgusted by this person I see in the mirror that I start crying. I can't help myself. Small tears at first, then big ones roll out of my eyes and down my cheeks, streaking the mascara and making the foundation all runny. It drips off my face in huge blobs, and my makeup is ruined. I sob hard, sitting in front of that mirror in the air-conditioned room, surrounded by the women of my family, who are all tsking and bemoaning my ungratefulness, until my face is a mess of the reds and browns and blacks they've painted on me. All their hard work of turning me into a pyaari woman is ruined. But thankfully, I get to wash it off.

VII.

This rigidity of gender follows me like a punishment every-where, across oceans and continents. Years later, in New York, a man spits at me as I walk past. "Are you a man or a woman?" he growls. I'm in a black hijab, a long-sleeved

T-shirt, and baggy boy jeans. It's an ordinary day and I'm in ordinary clothes chosen for maximal comfort. I turn around to look at him, surprised and wondering if he's talking to me. "Yeah, you," he says. I'm getting off the subway and he's walking in the other direction, walking away even as he says this. It's not a question he wants answered, it's just a statement, a statement deliberately meant to be an insult, laced with a violence that scares me. I turn back around, put my head down, and walk away as fast as I can.

"Excuse me, sir," the TSA agent says, and I keep walking through airport security because I don't realize he's talking to me. I'm wearing my favorite airport outfit: baggy jeans, a red hoodie, sneakers. *Sir*, he says louder and angrier, and another traveler taps my shoulder and points out that the TSA agent is trying to get my attention. The agent needs me to walk through the scanner again, needs me to take off my belt and hold my pants tighter. I will myself to stay calm. Should I correct him? Will the scanner show that I'm not a man? Is this technically deception? Can I get into trouble for this? I pass through the scanner the second time without it going off, grab my bags, and walk away quickly. I wait until I'm around the corner to sit down, put my head between my legs, and breathe deeply to slow down my racing heart.

My six-year-old cousin, who was born when I was twenty-two, whom I've been able to watch grow up—she's my uncle's daughter and his is the only family I have on this continent—tells me that when she was a baby, she thought I was a boy. She tells me that she didn't know I was a girl, but now she knows I'm a girl because her mom said so. She says this as she hands me a present that she made while I'm upstate visiting for the weekend: a drawing of me with my favorite blue hijab and glasses. Above the drawing, she has written in her adorably unsteady handwriting: "girl." She says she wrote it so that no one gets confused. "People can't tell you're a girl because you don't wear dresses, because your hair is short," she says. We have a long talk about how hair length doesn't make someone a girl or a boy, how there's no such thing as girl clothes or boy clothes, and sometimes people are neither. But isn't it interesting, I ask her, that the boys in our family don't pick up after themselves, that they're always saying mean things, that they get away with everything? This is where my aunt and uncle stop me and tell me that she's too young for feminist indoctrination, she's only a child, blah-blah-blah. I wait till later, when her parents aren't around, to fill her in on more.

VIII.

Of all the things I could be doing with my precious Saturday evening in New York, I'm standing in a long line to return clothes at a store. I hate shopping, but I have a new strategy to make the experience as painless as possible: I buy clothes online, try them on in the comfort of my home, and go to the store only to return anything that doesn't fit. It's frustrating to

have to stand under the glare of white lighting in a crowded
store on a Saturday evening, but it's the last day of my month-
long return window for these clothes. All of this is infinitely
better than the indignity of shopping in the men's section in
a hijab on a body that reads as woman. Shopping online, I can
avoid the stares from other customers, the alternatingly condescending or overly helpful salespeople, the fitting room
employees who flag me down afterward and say, "Miss, did
you know you were trying on men's jeans, would you like to
try on a women's pair that fit better?"

I'm waiting in this infinite line when I get a text from a
new friend asking where I am. We've been texting a lot, this
friend and me, after meeting recently at a college friend's
birthday. He's been friend-chasing me pretty hard and I like
being friend-chased. *I'm nearby,* he says, *can I come wait
with you?* I text back immediately, *Sure.* I'm always happy
for company, and he's easy to talk to, funny in a wry way, and
immeasurably kind. He shows up a few minutes later bearing a candy bar so I can have energy for my wait, regales me
with stories about white people in the Middle Eastern politics class he's taking, and transforms waiting in this line into
something much more fun. We catch each other up on our
days and then there is a lull in the conversation. All of a sudden, out of the blue and louder than I think he anticipated,
he says, "Hey, Lamya, do you bind?"

"Um, no?"

I'm embarrassed. I look around to see if anyone is listening to our conversation. Everyone looks pretty engrossed in
their phones, but that was definitely loud enough for the
entire store to hear.

"Well, if you ever need help, let me know. I wore binders for years before I got top surgery. I can give you a lot of really good tips."

I'm mortified to be talking about so intimate a topic loudly in line in a clothing store, with a person I don't actually know that well. I try to change the topic but he goes on for a while, talking about which brands of binders are great and where are the best places to get them, how they'll totally change the way I look in clothes. I make noncommittal noises until it's my turn at the counter. When I'm done with the transaction, he has thankfully forgotten what we were talking about.

Around 1 A.M. that night, he texts me. *I think you'd make a beautiful trans man. Have you ever thought about transitioning?*

I start laughing when I get his text. It's late and I've been procrastinating sleeping, so I'm a little loopy, and once I start laughing, I can't stop. The question feels so patronizing: as if I've never thought about gender and how I choose to present myself, how I dress, how I stand, how I crop my hair short, and what this means. As if I've never thought about what it would be like to live as a man instead, the relief that would come from passing, with not having to face the everyday violence and humiliations of living in my body. As if I've never thought about how I *don't* want that, how every cell in my body recoils at that thought of being a man, and yet how harrowing it is that the only way I can get out of my bed and make it through the day is by wearing masculinity on my body. As if I've never held dear my feminist rage, never thought about how I feel so politically aligned with womanhood and yet hate inhabiting it, hate it when my body is read as such. As if the only way to be trans is to transition to a binary gender, as if I can't exist as I have been, in some space in between or beyond, using she or they pronouns and seething when people call me a woman and laughing when people tell me I should transition.

I decide not to respond. The next morning, I wake up to another message from him, this one sent at 4 A.M.: ?—not even a sentence, just a question mark. I respond with a smiley face emoji, a purposefully deflective nonresponse that he must see through because he never brings it up again.

IX.

In the beginning, God created language and language is power and naming things is power and words like "he" or "she" or "they" are all power. The language God gave us hides meaning, adds meaning, and is constantly shifting beneath us, constantly creating our worlds and constantly creating us.

God knows this, of course. Describes divinity in ninety-nine names that expand language, that collide with the capacity of language to express. *Al-Qadir,* the One with Most Perfect Power Who Does Not Make Mistakes. *Al-Shaheed,* the All-Observing Witness. *Al-Haqq,* the Embodiment of Truth.

And gender is nowhere within these concepts that define the Divine. God is neither man nor woman nor masculine nor feminine, nor not masculine, nor not feminine. This God, who teaches us that we can be both and neither and all and beyond and capable of multiplicities and expansiveness. Nonbinary, genderqueer, They, this God that is the God, my God, my Allah. Who created the world and created language and created the first person, Adam, this first person who was man and woman and neither and both and not a mistake, never a mistake.

Like me.

PART
II

MUSA

I.

The first time I tell someone I'm queer, I do it without using words. There's no coming-out speech, no deliberating what phrases to use, no practicing out loud in front of the mirror—nothing like that. What happens instead is this: in the process of telling someone I'm queer, I end up telling myself.

It happens during college, on a summer trip. I've been hired to work as an English teacher in a country in Southeast Asia—a region of the world that I've never been to before. I'm with fourteen other students from my small elite school on this trip, a group that consists of one friend and thirteen strangers. We're teaching at a school in the countryside, surrounded by hills and streams and small towns. The campus is beautiful and idyllic, but there's no easy way to leave the walled compound we live and teach in—not on weekends, not in the evenings—and there's nowhere to go after class. Not that there's much we could do if we were able to leave the compound anyway; the closest city is two hours away, only two of us speak the language, and we'll be paid only at the end of the summer so we're all broke. *You don't need money, the school will provide you with everything you need,* the principal tells us on our first day of work. And they do. Three delicious meals a day, computers with unlimited dial-up internet, basketball courts, hiking trails, horses even. But still, it's hard not to feel trapped.

A consequence of being trapped is that the fifteen of us teaching at this school bond deeply. Not immediately, though. We spend the first two days making small talk with each other and unsuccessfully looking up bus routes that could take us to the nearest mall, the nearest grocery store, the nearest anywhere but here. The third day, we mourn— accepting the fact that we'll be each other's only company for the long summer ahead. By the fifth day, though, we are having intimate conversations—about our families, our traumas, God. About our hopes and dreams and the meaning we hope to derive from the lives ahead of us.

I'm both surprised and unsurprised at this bonding. I didn't expect to be absorbed into the group wholly. It's something I've never experienced before, the ease of this fitting in, how uncomplicatedly I'm able to osmose with the others now that we're all trapped, in this country where we're all foreign. And also, I'm unsurprised at the bonding, given the bunk beds in our communal dorm-style lodging at the school, the thin curtains between our shower stalls, the long table at which we eat our food and do our work and spend all our nonteaching hours.

It doesn't take too long for the intimacy of our arrangement to turn into a relishing of each other's company, and I hold my breath sometimes with the fear that I'll suddenly find myself on the outs in this group. That they'll discover things about me that they hate. That I'll say things or do things that are too weird, too different, too Muslim, too brown. But between these moments of doubt, I relish how easy it is to be around people who like each other, who like me. It's fun to spend all our free time together, hanging out and talking and playing cards. We're enjoying the endless hours of the summer nights, the languidness of nothing to do and nowhere to be. And I would be enjoying myself with abandon, except.

Except there's this girl. There's this girl on this trip for whom I have confusing feelings. I wasn't sure what they were at first, but now that we're about halfway through the summer, I'm pretty convinced what I'm feeling for this girl are *feelings*. Feelings that I'm not sure I have words for, though I do have more vocabulary than I did when I was pranking my economics teacher in high school, or when I had my realization about Maryam. I know that these feelings are some combination of attraction and curiosity and fascination. At first, it was only the latter: she's an athlete and grew up anomalously smart in small-town America— a combination that no one, including herself, knew quite how to handle. She's white, she's pretty, but this sense of being wrong has never left her, and she still carries herself like an outsider. I don't understand how she manages to be brilliant and brash and insecure at the same time. I am intrigued.

I want to figure her out, this girl, and I want to know everything about her. I'm conducting a character study, I tell myself at first. Once a week, the school charters a bus to a grocery store and I jostle my way into sitting next to her. Trapped for the twenty-minute ride, she indulges all my probing questions about her life. Later that night, at dinner, she saves me a seat at the big table and surprises me with probing questions of her own. As the trip goes on, we trade books and banter, even swap shampoo over the top of our favorite shower stalls that are right next to each other. She laughs at all my jokes, even the dumb ones, even the ones that don't have a punch line. I find it enthralling that she's willing to jump headlong into talking about hard things she knows nothing about.

Like race. One night, as we're all sitting on the porch under the stars, this girl calls me a "cutie brownie."

"Uh-oh," says my friend Cara, who is also white. She is my closest friend on this trip, the one person I knew before coming here, and the kindest person I know. Ever since she switched her major to gender studies, she has become an incredible ally. "You can't say that," Cara says to this girl.

"What? Why? Lamya is cute, Lamya is brown, *and* Lamya likes brownies!" the girl says, and I find her earnestness adorable.

"Um, because of white privilege?" I say. With all the self-righteousness of our early twenties, Cara and I walk her through why there are certain things she can't say as a white person, teach her phrases that are more acceptable to use like *South Asian* and *people of color,* try to explain the invisible knapsack of whiteness that affords her opportunities that others will never have. And this girl shuts up and listens and reflects. Then she tells us about how horribly the only two kids of color in her high school—both East Asian— were treated, draws connections to how often her Black roommate is harassed in stores. After she's done talking, we fall silent, reveling in the satisfaction of getting through to her. Until she pipes up again.

"But what I still don't understand is why I can't call Lamya a cutie brownie."

She drives me nuts, this girl. I know that she doesn't currently have a boyfriend, but I wonder if she ever has. She has this energy about her that makes it hard to imagine her with a guy, has some of this swagger that reminds me of the lesbians I play soccer with. But also, she knows nothing about gay people, claims to not know any "homosexuals," doesn't even know that rugby, which she played in high school, has traditionally been a safe haven for women who love women. I'm pretty sure she's straight.

I can't decipher her, and at first, I was convinced that my interest was a blend of admiration and confusion. But after a few weeks have gone by, I'm pretty sure these feelings are something else, the inconvenient feelings I've had for women before. Feelings I've been hoping are a phase, something nebulous that I'll never have to address, something that I'll outgrow and never have to deal with the repercussions of, never have to even name. But these feelings don't seem to be going away and they're becoming harder to ignore, because I want to be around this girl all the time and, being trapped, I *get* to be around her all the time.

I hold these feelings inside the contours of myself until

one night, I just can't. All night, at dinner, this girl has told me to open my mouth as she feeds me piece after piece of my favorite pickled ginger condiment. The tenderness is too much, and it becomes too hard to hold these feelings inside me. It's late by the time we're done with dinner, and half of the group drifts onto the porch. People are settling into low chairs and talking to each other in the blanket of the dark, and I intercept Cara before she can join them.

"Do you have a moment?" I say to her quickly, softly. "I kinda need to talk to you about something."

"Of course!" Cara says. She's great at taking things like this in stride. Says her good nights to everyone and motions for me to follow her. She leads me to a rickety side staircase, up to a shallow balcony that's quiet and still. We're a few floors above the porch; stray voices and giggles float up to us, but we're high up enough for the treetops to dampen the sounds. It feels like we're the only two people in the world, the inky sky stretched out above us, dark blue with streaks of pink.

"What did you want to talk about?" Cara asks.

I fiddle. First with the keys in my pocket, then with the carvings on the railing, with the cords on my sweatshirt. I still don't know what I'm going to say, still don't know what feels true enough to put into words, but the taste of pickled ginger is still in my mouth and everything reminds me of the girl, every swallow, every breath.

Cara doesn't say anything, just waits. Gently, so gently, like we have all the time in the world. I compose half sentences in my head, try out and discard different words. I draw in a breath like I'm going to start talking, but no words come out so I reset and try again, fail again. I'm about to chicken out, when I hear her, this girl, her unmistakable laugh from the porch underneath us, and it's too much, too much to carry these feelings inside me. It sort of spills out.

"I think I kinda like someone," I say. It feels so big for what it is, this admission that admits nothing.

"I figured that was it," Cara says. "Is it Mike?"

There are two boys on this trip. Mike is the one who is starting to get on everyone's nerves, the one who has a weird fetish for the women in the country we're in, who has been pushy and annoying and just such a dude.

"No, no. Definitely not. Absolutely not."

Cara draws in a quick breath. "Is it Matt?"

Matt is the boy Cara kinda sorta likes, whom she's been kinda sorta flirting with, who's been kinda sorta flirting back. Matt is the only other boy on this trip.

"No."

Cara is visibly relieved, while I grow visibly tense. And then something else passes across her face. Something very, very gentle.

"Is it a girl?" she says in a voice that strikes me as impressively nonchalant.

I don't say anything. Later on, I'll remember my body shaking. Later on, I'll remember that I couldn't even look at Cara. In the moment, though, I feel like I'm somewhere outside and above my body, like the only thing keeping me tethered to this balcony are the thin soles of my flip-flops. I'm scared. All I have to say is one word: yes. One word that will turn my feelings into something real, something tangible, something with a name. And yet. This one word is stuck in my throat. I don't say anything, I can't. Instead, I tremble. Caught on the brink, I pause.

A man and a woman and their children travel through the desert, returning home to Egypt after decades of exile. It's cold, it's dark, and they're tired. Tired of long nights walking, of long days waiting for the heat to break, of traveling, of each other. Suddenly, they see a light in the distance. It's a little weird, this light: pale, not quite the color of fire, not quite *not* the color of fire, but still distinct, distinctly there. The man, Musa, says he'll go investigate. "Maybe there are people there," he says, "Maybe I can talk to them, maybe they'll guide me a little, or maybe they'll give me some of their fire." The woman, his wife, Safurah, encourages him to go. She is thankful for the break—from Musa, from walking. She is thankful for the potential of warmth.

Musa walks toward this light. It is strange, this blaze burning atop a mountain. No one else is around, no people, no animals, no tents. Nothing but this flame. He approaches carefully, fearfully. And as he grows closer, a deep voice booms out. *Musa,* this voice says. *I am your God.*

Musa is too stunned to speak. This fire in the middle of the desert is God?

Yes, I am your God, the voice says, reading his mind. *And I have chosen you.*

"Me?" Musa squeaks.

Yes, you. You are a prophet now. And I need you to listen to My commands. Worship Me, pray to Me, do good to others.

Teach others this creed and establish justice on this earth. To do that, I need you to overthrow your adopted father, the pharaoh who rules Egypt.

Musa is speechless. He is shy before this God and totally overwhelmed.

God tries again, talks to him more gently this time. *What are you holding in your hand?*

"It's just a stick. I lean on it, I use it to guide my sheep, and use it for lots of other things."

Throw it down, God says.

Musa is perplexed, but he does as he's told. The stick turns into a snake. Writhing, hissing, a real live snake.

Now pick it up, God says.

Musa wavers, does not want to touch this snake.

Don't be afraid, God says. *It'll be okay. I got you. Listen to me. Trust me. I chose you. I have your back.*

And this man, chosen by God, is terrified. How can he not be? He's being told by a voice in a fire to pick up a live snake. In the middle of the desert, no help, no nothing, his family waiting for him to get back and no one around for miles.

Musa trembles. Caught on the brink, he pauses.

Then he takes a deep breath and gathers up his courage and does it. Just does it, picks up the snake, and the snake turns back into a stick. It's a miracle, a miracle from God.

This is your miracle, says God. *Now go forth. Tell the pharaoh I sent you. Tell him you're a prophet. Defeat him and save the people he's oppressing.*

The words that come out of Musa next are my favorite duaa, a prayer that comes to my lips again and again when I don't have words of my own. "My Lord. Expand for me my breast with confidence. And ease for me my task. And untie the knot from my tongue. That my speech may be understood."

And then, in the miracles and events that follow, God helps Musa. God answers.

And I, on the brink, am scared. Cara is asking me if I like girls, and here it is, this moment when I'm supposed to say yes, because the answer is yes, has always been yes. But I tremble. I pause. And say Musa's prayer in my head. *My Lord. Expand for me my breast with confidence. And ease for me my task. And untie the knot from my tongue. That my speech may be understood.*

I take a deep breath and gather up my courage and just do it. By which I mean, I nod in answer to Cara's question.

"Oh! I totally know who you like! And let me tell you, she's really hot. She kind of reminds me of Ava, who I had a crush on last year."

And Cara says some other stuff in the same breath, more stuff about Ava, about what it felt like to realize that she had a crush on a girl, and she's speaking so casually, and I didn't even know that Cara liked girls, but it's exactly what I need in this moment, the nonchalance and normalness of it all. I feel so relieved, so much lighter after telling her, after telling myself. Not being alone with this revelation is not just enough. It's everything.

I pray that night for God to help me like he helped

Musa, in all that will follow this moment. This moment of receiving this miracle, my miracle from God.

II.

The first time I tell family I'm queer, it's not even my own family I come out to, it's my friend's. I'm at dinner with one of my besties, Billy, at our favorite dosa place in New York a year after graduating from college, the two of us ensconced in the window table at the restaurant where we eat every Thursday night. It's raining outside and bustling inside; the windows around our corner are foggy, wrapping us in a soft cocoon. Billy waits until my belly is full of carbs before making his plea.

"Hey, Lamya, I want to talk to you about something. Is there any chance you can do me a solid and tell my parents you're queer?"

"Wait, what?" I say, caught off guard. It's been two years since I came out to Cara, and I've come out to a handful of close friends since then, six or seven at the most. Billy was the first person I told in New York—we were in the same program in grad school and I hadn't known him very long, but something about this openly queer femme white boy from a small rural town in the South felt familiar, and I knew, I just knew that we were going to be friends for a very long time. But even now, after having told Cara and Billy and having all this practice telling people, I'm still hesitant about sharing something so intimate about myself with oth-

ers. Each time I tell someone feels like a complicated calcu-
lation. Why am I telling this person? Will I derive emotional
support from them? Will I have to do a lot of explaining?
Can I trust that this person won't tell others? Can I trust
that it won't get back to my parents, my Muslim community,
my classmates in grad school? Even now, at this restaurant,
I'm hesitant to talk about queerness in such a public space.
I look around quickly to see who could overhear us, scan
the faces of the diners around us for anyone who might look
vaguely familiar from my mosque or school. But no one is
paying us any attention. I release the breath I didn't even
realize I was holding.

"Okay, I know it's hard for you to tell people you're gay,
but please don't say no before hearing my full argument,"
Billy says.

I raise my eyebrow. "I'm listening, but just so you know:
the answer is still going to be no way, absolutely not, nope,
no."

"But you know how people are always giving you advice
on how to be gay? And telling you that you have to come out
to your parents?"

"Yes?"

"What if you came out to mine instead? To have that
authentically gay experience?"

I groan.

Not at Billy—at all the people and blogs that have given
me unbidden advice about how to be authentically gay. The
most elusive of all these experiences, the one I'm most often
told I must do immediately, is some version of this: I need
to come out to my parents. I need to tell them that I'm gay

and then I'll cry, they'll cry. They'll hug me and reiterate their love, tell me that I'm brave, that love is love, that it's going to get better, that it's going to be okay. And if it doesn't work out like that, if my parents don't accept me for who I am, then I'm supposed to walk away from them. My parents will eventually come around and everything will be fine, or they'll never come around and I should cut them out of my life forever. Easy peasy, the end.

As if it would be that easy to tell my parents, as if it even feels possible. My parents, who live across an ocean in a country where queerness operates so differently, isn't openly discussed, isn't an identity. My parents, who don't know any openly queer people. Who have only heard about homosexuality as sin, as disease, as something that must not be named. What would my telling them I'm queer achieve? My parents would see it as a failure of their parenting. I could never do that to these people who birthed me, who left their families to build a more comfortable life for me in a country where they didn't know anyone and didn't even know the language. I wouldn't be able to be there for them as they struggled with the knowledge of my queerness. I wouldn't be able to hold them, wouldn't be able to tell them that I still love them, that I'm still the same me. My parents wouldn't get it and they wouldn't have anyone around them who'd get it, either: not friends, not family, no peer-support groups, nothing. They wouldn't even have the words to understand my queerness, words that aren't derogatory in the language we speak to each other. How does it make any sense to tell them I'm queer? While we're so far away from each other, while borders and visas keep them from visiting me, while they don't even know my everyday life? I'm not planning to come out to my parents, not now and possibly not ever. It doesn't make sense.

All of which I find myself constantly having to explain to people. In a bookstore on a snowy day a few months after moving to New York, I was browsing the LGBTQ books section with a friend from college whom I'd recently come out to, when she asked me how my parents were doing.

"Still struggling with empty-nest syndrome now that my brother moved out and I'm trying to convince them to get a cat, but otherwise they're doing well."

"No, silly, how are they doing with you coming out to them?" she said as the snow started to come down faster outside the window behind her.

"Um, I haven't come out to them. And I'm not planning to."

I was genuinely confused why she was asking. She was brown, too, though not Muslim, and identified as bisexual. We'd never talked before about me coming out to my parents; I'd never thought I'd need to justify not coming out to them to her.

"You know, mine were only upset for like two days when I told them I was bi," she said. I remembered when she was figuring out how to frame this to her family. I remembered that she had decided to couple her coming out with telling them that she was engaged to her brown boyfriend, that her parents were upset about her sexuality but ecstatic that she wanted to marry a cis straight brown guy in medical school.

"You should tell your parents, too, Lamya, so you can come out to the world," my friend told me. "You owe this visibility to the queer community. You need to be out to lead an authentically gay life!"

"I'll think about it," I remember saying as we buttoned our coats to brave the world outside, which the snow had whitened anew.

Her argument was far from being the only one I'd heard over the past two years. At soccer practice the summer before grad school, I ended up next to my favorite teammate during the last ten minutes when we were doing core exercises. She was so comfortable in her gayness, this teammate, so visibly queer, so unafraid to be herself. It was hard not to absorb some of that energy when I was around her, so when she had casually asked me a few weeks before that if I was into women, I found myself saying yes, surprised at how easy it felt—this one simple word I hadn't been able to utter to Cara the year before. We hadn't talked a lot about it since, but that day at practice, she started telling me about this bartender she had a crush on.

"Hey, what are you doing Friday night? Want to come with me to this lesbian bar?" she said between sets of sit-ups.

"Mm, no, thanks," I said as I struggled to catch my breath, the Astroturf tickling my back.

"Why not? The music at this place is poppin' and we can play wingman for each other!"

"It's not really my scene . . ." I said, except the "not really" part was not exactly true, I knew it was definitely not my scene. Cara had dragged me there once after a Pride event. As we waited in line that sweltering day, I had felt someone behind me stroking my striped blue hijab. When I

had turned around, the woman had leered at me. *Nice,* she
had said, drawing out the word. I wanted to leave right then,
but Cara had convinced me to stay. "Ignore her! There are
always stupid people everywhere, but I promise it'll be better inside," she had said, but it hadn't been better inside. I
had felt so out of place in this bar filled with smoke and too-
loud music, with palpable sexual tension and sly checkouts
and an endlessly sticky floor. I could see how it would be
other people's scene, though: Cara had come alive when we
had entered the bar, absorbed the vibe of the room, and had
danced with curls flying. I watched the transformation,
mesmerized, from where I was sitting holding our table. I
had twiddled with my phone and slowly sipped my ginger
ale until it was a respectable time to say good night to Cara,
whom I found flirting in the bathroom line with a cutie, and
then I had left. Definitely not my scene.

"Listen," my teammate had said as we ended our work-
out and jogged to grab our water bottles. "Even if you can't
make it on Friday, you should still come hang out at this bar
with me sometime! It's the best place to meet other lesbians. Do it for the culture! How else are you going to be gay?"

But there must be other ways to be authentically gay.
One evening, at a queer poetry reading that Billy dragged
me to at the LGBTQ center, I thought I'd found an alternative. I hadn't wanted to go at first, all the poets in the lineup
were white and I wasn't sure I "understood" poetry. But the
reading was better than I had anticipated. I'd never before
heard poems that moved me so much, poems about loss,
grieving childhoods that folks never got to experience, about

longing and desire and how the straights are not okay. I
learned how to snap my fingers at the good parts, how to
hum at lines that I particularly liked. I found myself swept
up in the collective experience of the crowd experiencing
the words. It was magical. I felt maybe even a little authentically gay.

But then, after a short Q and A with the poets, Billy ran
to the bathroom and I told him I'd gather our stuff and meet
him at the door. As I was getting up, the two white women
sitting next to us struck up a conversation with me. They
were older, in their early fifties maybe, and they asked me
how I heard of this event, who my favorite readers of the
night were, and other small talk things.

Then one of the women said, "If you don't mind me asking, me and my partner were curious. How do you identify?"

"Oh!" I said. "I mean, I moved around a lot as a kid and
I'm not sure I identify with any place; sometimes I say I'm
generically brown or South Asian."

The two women looked at each other. "Sorry for being
nosy, we meant in terms of sexuality."

I was caught off guard. As if my being at the LGBTQ
center, experiencing the poetry alongside them all evening
wasn't enough, as if I still needed to prove that I was gay. As
if I needed to be anything, as if I needed to define myself to
be legible. Luckily, despite my anger, my deflection skills
were intact. I asked them how *they* identified, and when
they said lesbian, I asked about why that word and not
queer, and they went into a long rant about words that are
currently fashionable that were not around when they were

coming out. By that time, Billy came back from the bathroom and rescued me. We were making our escape when one of the women stopped me.

"Thank you," she said, holding my hand and looking me in the eye. "Thank you for being such a good ally."

Billy was livid when I told him what happened while he was in the bathroom. I told him how people have been trying to tell me how to be authentically gay, and it made him angrier. "We'll do gay things together," he said, and lived up to his promise with things we decided were gay enough: dosas every Thursday evening; watching the soccer World Cup and picking which teams to cheer for based on anti-imperialism; cooking brussels sprout pasta; walking his dog. Billy has never pressured me to do authentically gay things before, so I don't understand why he is now, over dosas, trying to convince me to come out to his parents.

"Okay, fine. I have an ulterior motive for why I want you to tell my parents you're gay," Billy says. He pauses dramatically. I'm used to his dramatic pauses and keep eating my dosa.

"My parents think you're in love with me."

"What?" I spit out the bite I was attempting to chew. This, I did not see coming. His parents were just here visiting a few weeks ago. They took me with them to the U.S. Open because they had an extra ticket and then invited me to a barbecue at Billy's place. Nowhere in the hours and hours we spent together did they let on that they thought this.

"You heard right. They sat me down before they left and told me you're in love with me."

I can't get any more words out. I'm laughing so hard that I start to cough, and our favorite waiter comes over to check in on us and makes me promise to drink more water.

"I know, I know," Billy says. "But it's not so funny when your parents won't shut up about how your friend is in love with you. Now they're hounding me about it every time we talk on the phone."

"Did you tell them I'm not in love with you?"

"I tried! You don't understand. I told them we're just friends. I told them that I know for a fact that you're not into me. But they won't stop. They said that I'm being dense. That your eyes light up when you look at me. That anyone with a brain can tell you're in love with me."

It's true, I do love him. I love his brilliance, his kindness, that I can text him whenever to rant about whatever and whoever. That we understand each other's anxieties and fears, that we read the same articles and blogs and books. I know we confuse more than his parents when we're hanging out: me, with my brown skin, hijab, and boy jeans; him with his flamboyance, white-blond hair, and fashionista drop-crotch pants. But it's frustrating that these are the only things people see about us and cannot see past. Why can't people see the everyday overlaps of our lives? Difficult work situations and queer shame. The newfound deliciousness of frozen yogurt. Navigating the uncannily similar experiences of Irish Catholic guilt and brown diasporic guilt. Instead, it's only the contrasts that people see. One time, after a particularly spirited argument in the elevator about whether or not toast is a white-people thing, an acquaintance who was eavesdropping earnestly told us that it must be hard to reconcile our "cultural differences." It's no wonder that his parents can only understand our friendship as unrequited love.

"I'm not sure about this whole coming-out-to-your-parents thing," I tell Billy, signaling to the waiter for our check. "But I promise I'll think about it. Now can we get frozen yogurt?"

Billy calls me a few weeks later, on Christmas Eve. I'm moping in my apartment, still in pajamas in the late afternoon. I'm glad to hear from him; he's been at his childhood home for the past few days, and I've missed him.

"Listen, Lamya," he says as soon as I pick up. "My parents are at it again. My sister showed them that photo of us from Halloween when we dressed in each other's clothes and now they won't stop saying you're in love with me." His voice is crackly with desperation.

"Did you tell them that you told me that they think I'm in love with you? That I laughed so hard the waiter looked ready to do the Heimlich?"

"Yes! But then they got mad at me for telling you! They think I'm setting you up for heartbreak."

I giggle.

"Please, Lamya. Can you come out to them? I can't take any more of this."

I'm feeling magnanimous on this rare day off from grad school when I don't even have to change out of my pajamas, and instead of automatically shutting Billy down again, I pause. Who will his parents tell? They live in a small town on the other side of the country from everyone I know. What do I have to lose? If anything, I could gain an authentically gay experience.

"Okay. Let's do it," I say, and then sigh dramatically. "The things I do for you . . ."

"Thank you. I owe you frozen yogurt," he says, sounding relieved.

Billy video chats me a few minutes later, from the living room of the house he grew up in. He's sitting at a table with his mom, both in matching Christmas sweaters with a giant wreath behind them. His mom is, as always, incredibly affectionate and delighted to talk to me. Asks me how I'm doing, how my holidays are, how work is going. Before I lose my courage, I draw on every cliché I've heard of and begin.

When Musa gets to Egypt, he does what God tells him to do. God is so convincing, how could Musa not? The day he arrives, he goes straight to Pharaoh's court.

"I'm here to overthrow you," Musa says. "Stop your tyranny, stop oppressing my people. I'm here to take them away."

Pharaoh laughs. His courtesans laugh. Their laughter booms out through the cavernous hall and shakes the furniture, the curtains, the trees in the garden.

"You?" Pharaoh says. "You're an orphan that came to my palace in a basket from the river. You think you can overthrow me?"

"God has sent me to you," says Musa.

"I am God," says Pharaoh.

"No, you are not God. God is the one Who made everything on the earth, Who made us all out of the earth and will return us to it when we die."

"I don't believe you," says Pharaoh. "No one will believe you. If you're really a prophet, you must prove it."

"Here is this miracle God gave me," Musa says. He throws down his stick. It turns into a snake again, writhing and hissing. "Look at this. Here is proof."

"Oh, that?" says Pharaoh. "It's just magic. Let's call the other magicians. You'll see that no one will believe you."

A showdown is arranged: Musa versus all the magicians in the land. Word spreads. The magicians have been promised a reward for defeating Musa. The day of the event, a large crowd gathers. People are curious about this Musa, who claims to be sent by God.

"Do you want to go first or shall we?" ask the magicians.

"You go," says Musa.

The magicians throw down sticks and ropes that look like snakes. Writhing, hissing snakes. Musa is scared anew. He doesn't know how his miracle will hold up to this test, but then he hears God's voice again in his head. *Throw down your stick. This is real. I have your back.*

Musa throws down his stick and it turns into a snake, a real snake that swallows up the magicians' false snakes. The magicians bow down. They have been defeated. They know this is no magic, that it's a miracle from God. They fall down in prostration. "We believe in the God of Musa," they say.

Pharaoh is enraged. He yells and threatens, swears that he will torture the magicians and have them crucified. The magicians won't budge. They believe.

And other people believe, too. Musa works slowly,

steadily. Gets to know the people in his community and gains their trust and then, only then, invites them to God. The people who are the most marginalized, the most oppressed come first. They're the most receptive to Musa and his ideas on justice. They're interested in liberation, in freeing themselves and each other from the horrific edicts of Pharaoh, from the oppression that they're facing. And slowly Musa invites others, too, who are interested in this growing community, this group of people building together. He invites them in, and they follow.

"I have something to tell you," I say to Billy's mom. "I don't think it'll come as a big surprise, but I think it's time that I share this with you. I really hope you can still love me when you know this, I hope this doesn't change anything about our relationship."

"Of course. Is everything okay?" her face is soft, suddenly concerned.

Before I can change my mind, I say it: "I'm gay."

There's an awkward pause while Billy's mom's eyes go wide. My words seem to reverberate on the slightly staticky line.

"Oh!" she finally says. Her eyes somehow widen even more. I try again.

"I love your son! You're not wrong, I love him, but not like *that*. I'm not in love with him. I'm gay."

"Duh," Billy's sister, who will later come out as queer, pipes up in the background. I let out the giggle I've been holding inside me.

"Oh." His mom says, "Oh, okay." It takes her a few seconds, but she composes herself and says all the things you're supposed to, the usual assurances: we love you, thank you for sharing, it's so brave of you to tell us, to background taunts of *I told you so!* and *Hah!* from Billy.

We hang up, and it's funny, I don't feel different, don't feel gayer. If this is supposed to be the authentically gay experience, it doesn't work. Everything feels pretty much the same.

A little later, I text Billy to ask how his mom is doing, how she's taking it. He texts back immediately. *I thought she got it, I really thought she did. But she's still telling me you're in love with me. She said it's probably because—and I'm quoting her here—you're "a bisexual."*

We crack up at her antiquated use of "a" before bisexual, we laugh really hard at the fact that she doesn't believe me. But underneath, I can't help feeling heartbroken. That after years of confusion, wanting to die, ignoring my feelings for women until I couldn't anymore, finally coming out to myself by coming out to Cara and feeling so much relief that I knew I'd experienced a miracle—that even after all of this, my saying the truth out loud is not enough to prove who I am to a world that doesn't believe me.

III.

The first time I own my queerness without apology, I don't mean to; I stumble into it.

It happens at a doctor's office. There are only a few

certified doctors in the city that do the kind of medical examination I need for my immigration forms. The medical exam starts off easy, just like an annual physical: blood tests and vaccines and questions about my health. And then suddenly becomes increasingly invasive and uncomfortable. Questions about mental health, drug use, STIs, asking the doctor to assess whether or not I'll engage in "harmful behavior," whether I'll be a burden to society.

The entire thing seems specifically designed to be terrifying. That I even need a medical examination for my immigration forms is terrifying. That my ability to stay in this country is dependent on a special doctor who can sign and seal and swear to tell the truth is terrifying—as if the decades of student visas, years of employment authorizations that expire every twelve months, visa stamps that must be renewed when I leave the country—as if all of this hasn't been terrifying enough. It looms over me that a mistaken medical omission could jeopardize my ability to live here. I feel like immigration agents are looking over my shoulder when I'm printing the forms, gathering all my vaccination records, carefully picking out my clothes for the doctor's appointment. I'm hyperaware of myself and my body, hyperaware that I need to choose my outfit so I come across as not just competent and organized, but also well adjusted, physically healthy, mentally sound.

So I fall back on what I know, the small rituals I practice before all of my school exams. Organize all my notes and printouts beforehand and check through them the morning of. Eat a big breakfast, pray two rakat nafl before leaving the house and depart early enough for an unhurried commute. I arrive at the office half an hour before my appointment. The bored receptionist leisurely checks me in and directs me to a seat in the foyer. I sit up straight in a hard-backed plastic chair clutching my files, next to a woman with a runny nose, and wait. In this too-small room with drab gray walls and the sharp smell of cleaning alcohol, what I really want to do is jog in place, do some jumping jacks, burn off some of this fear-induced energy that is coursing through me. Instead, I sit and wait.

It doesn't help that I hate doctors. Their condescending manner, their brashness, and their tendency to touch and prod and ask personal questions. But the doctor who calls me into her office is browner than I'd expected from her anglicized name. The way she says my name—short first syllable and emphasis on the second—makes me pretty sure she's Arab. Instead of intimidating, she seems sweet and kind. She's around my mother's age and is tiny; I'm average height, but I tower over her as I follow her into her office. It's brightly lit via two giant windows and is remarkably cheery for a doctor's office, full of plants and colorful, geometric, unmistakably Islamic art. She asks me to sit down—in a normal chair, not on one of those awkward paper-lined tables. From this angle, I can see the edges of a homely floral dress peeking out underneath her white coat, her hair combed over a bald spot. She's an aunty doctor.

I'm disarmed and feel instantly relieved. The aunty doctor is chatty, starts telling me about her daughter who's the same age as me, interrupts her own stream of chatter to answer the phone and speaks into it in a thick Egyptian Arabic dialect. I grew up around Egyptian aunties, going to Egyptian aunty doctors. The contours of her mannerisms are deeply familiar. She reminds me of my neighbors, my friends' moms, my mom. I'm beginning to feel like I'm at home.

Of course, the defining feature of aunties is that they think they can run your life. When she hangs up the phone, she turns to me. Looks me up and down.

"You know, you shouldn't wear black. It doesn't go with your dark skin tone."

"Okay?"

"And I can already tell by your coloring that you're anemic. You should eat more meat."

"I'm vegetarian."

"That's fine. But you need to throw some beef into your food now and then."

"Okay." I laugh, deciding to keep it light and pretend that she's joking—the best that I can do in this particular power dynamic—but my armor is up again, more quickly than it had come down. I remind myself to breathe, to tamp down my frustration. Luckily, the aunty doctor starts filling out the form and asking me about vaccinations, my medical history, my parents' medical history. She gets to the section about the tests she has to order, asks if I'm scared of drawing blood, if she needs to order a pregnancy test in case the tuberculosis skin test is inconclusive and a chest X-ray is required.

"There's no need for that, I'm not pregnant," I say.

"Are you sure? Sometimes people are more pregnant than they think."

I laugh and respond without thinking. "I'm *definitely* not pregnant."

It must be a special aunty skill to be able to root out the meaning of what's left unsaid, because she puts her pen down, stops flipping through the forms, and looks up.

"How are you so sure?" she asks.

I hesitate. Even now, a decade after I came out, a decade spent building a queer life, I hesitate. I hadn't anticipated this aunty doctor, hadn't anticipated my careless answer, and I don't have a game plan for navigating this immigration situation in which I legally have to tell the truth in response to this question that will out me.

"Lamya," she says again. "I asked how you know you're not pregnant?"

Musa collects a community of those who believe in his God and his miracles, then God tells Musa to leave. *Enough is enough,* God says. *Pharaoh is a tyrant and will never change, it's time for you to leave Egypt with your followers and move to a blessed land.* Musa is ready; his life has been too transient, too unstable, too in-between, and he's ready to leave and start over, to put down roots and start building a life.

So he gathers his people, his band of believers. Tells them God's plan. They're going to travel light, gather their most valuable possessions and some provisions, and sneak away in the middle of the night. It'll be a difficult journey through an unforgiving desert, but they'll settle somewhere nice. They'll find a new place and build themselves a home.

Pharaoh, of course, has spies everywhere. He finds out about this plan and is infuriated. Gathers his people, his armed acolytes, his militias, and sets chase after Musa. Positions his army so Musa and his followers are surrounded with nowhere to go except into the Red Sea. Pharaoh closes in slowly, cunningly. Where are Musa and his people going to go, with armies on three sides and the water on the fourth?

Musa turns to the water. It's too deep, too wide to cross with his people. And they can't surrender now. Pharaoh is ruthless, he'll kill them all. This is it. It's over—his dreams of safety, of stability. This is how it'll all end.

Except it doesn't. God talks to Musa from above. *It'll be okay,* God says. *I got you. Listen to me. Trust me. I chose you. I have your back.*

God tells Musa to throw his stick into the water. And Musa hesitates, but then he throws the stick boldly. The sea parts into two giant towers of waves, held back by God. The sea has become passable and Musa and his people run across to safety. Pharaoh and his army chase them into the chasm left by the sea, but God closes the sea up over them and they drown. Musa and his people are already on the other side. Safe.

And me. A girl who grew up in a city on the sea. Sitting before this doctor filling out immigration forms, holding the life I've built, the queer life that I'm building, in her hands. I could deflect or lie or refuse to answer, but it strikes me:

What if I didn't? What if I told the truth? After a decade of calculating when it is and isn't safe to come out, of people assuming I'm straight, of never feeling authentically gay enough, I feel tired. Or reckless. Or maybe brave. *What would Musa do?* I think. *What would Maryam do?* I take a deep breath and meet her gaze.

"I'm definitely not pregnant because I'm gay."

The doctor looks at me coolly, taking in my hijab and butch clothes. "Do your parents know?"

"No."

"Oh. They must be so confused."

I'm too brown to blush, but I feel all my blood rush to my face.

"Do you drink? Or do drugs?"

Those questions I know are on the form, but it still feels like I'm being tested. "No."

"Tell me something. Why? What kind of gay are you? Why do you still veil?"

My skin crawls, not with humiliation but with anger. What does it matter that I'm gay? That I'm not out to my parents? That I wear hijab and don't participate in a particular kind of gay nightlife culture? This is the kind of gay I've grown into, this is what my queerness looks like and I have nothing to prove.

Thankfully, God saves me from answering the aunty doctor's question. The phone rings and she picks up. When she's done, she seems distracted by her conversation on the phone and forgets what we were talking about. Finishes filling out the rest of the forms quickly and hands them over.

And just like that, the medical exam is over. I pass. I

have owned my queerness, and in doing so, accepted it for what it is: a miracle. A difficult miracle, like Musa's. One that I didn't ask for, had no choice but to receive. Sent from God, who made the heavens and the earth and who does not make mistakes. God, who has my back. God, who answered.

MUHAMMAD

I.

You. You're forty years old when you receive the wahi, a revelation from God in the form of a command. *Read.*

It comes unexpectedly, on an ordinary night. A dark night, a quiet night, clear and still. You're alone. Meditating, as you periodically do, in a cave on a mountain overlooking the desert. A quilt of lanterns lighting up the city below you, the stars lighting up the skies above. An ordinary night in your ordinary life, one that began with extraordinary grief: the death of your father a few months before you were born; the death of your mother when you were a child; the death of your grandfather who took over providing for you. But in the years since, you've built a life for yourself: a job you love, raising sheep; a wife you love, who loves you back. And periodically this, this time to yourself: meditating in a cave you love outside a city you love. A city that loves you back, that knows you as one of its own. Knows you as a man who is gentle, who is kind. As al-sadiq: the honest. As al-ameen: the trustworthy. As someone who lives his name: Muhammad, meaning he who is deserving of praise.

But on this ordinary night, everything changes. You're meditating in a cave and God sends you an angel. In the form of a voice at first, just one word of the wahi booming into the silence and surrounding you. *Read*. You're sure you're imagining it. There is no one around for miles and miles. But there it is again, this voice that is everywhere, that envelops you and squeezes all the air out of your chest. *Read*. And then, you see it. This unearthly being that is completely out of the ordinary. *Read*. It approaches you, descending from the sky, this angel that is Gabriel himself, with wings so large they shroud the sky and extinguish all light. *Read*, the angel says, and you're shaking with fear. You're unlettered and you don't know how to read, but the angel says it again and again. *Read*.

"What should I read?" you ask, terrified and confused, and that is when your life changes, on this ordinary night, the night you get the wahi. A revelation from God, these first few verses of the Quran—of which there will be many more over the course of the next two decades. Verses on faith, verses on enacting justice, verses about prophets before you. Thousands of verses on subjects you've never been taught—embryology, astronomy, inheritance law; on topics you never could have imagined yourself preaching about, you who can't even read. Verses that your followers will learn and teach and assemble into a text, will distribute to lands you'll never see, in centuries long after you're dead.

But for now, the wahi is only a few verses and they are all commands. To read, to rise, to not be afraid. To teach good, to forbid evil. To warn people that the day of judgment will come, bringing justice for those who have been wronged. To end oppression: of the poor, of the marginalized, of women. To teach Islam, to teach the message of God, one God, Allah. Allah, who revealed the wahi.

You run down the mountain that night when you receive the wahi, that night your life changes. You run to your home, to your wife, Khadijah. "What's wrong?" she asks. You're terrified of what has happened, and you're terrified to tell her. Will she think you're crazy? Will she think you're possessed? What has happened is so out of the ordinary, will she even believe you?

"Cover me, cover me," you say, your teeth clattering, your body trembling. She wraps you in a heavy blanket to soothe you.

Eventually, you feel calm enough to tell Khadijah what has transpired, about the angel, the voice, the commands, your terror.

"I'm afraid," you say. "I'm scared something bad is going to happen."

Khadijah listens to you patiently, without judgment. When she responds, she is measured and thoughtful. "Don't be afraid. Allah will not let anything bad happen to you. You are kind to your loved ones. You are truthful. You help those in need. Don't be afraid, something new is happening. And Allah will take care of you."

You are forty years old when you hear this, and it's exactly what you need, these words of comfort and support, the knowledge that someone believes you and has your back. This is what you'll need as you start venturing into the world, spreading the message of Islam and building a community of believers.

And I. I am twenty-one when I come out to myself as queer, when I receive something akin to a wahi of my own. I spend years afraid, like Muhammad, that something bad is around the corner. That I'll trust the wrong person with the truth about my queerness and just like that, everything I've built will crumble: my life, my relationship with my family, my ability to practice faith among other Muslims. But like Muhammad, I have people who offer words of comfort and support, who believe me and have my back. This is what I'll need as I, too, start venturing into the world—to live as a queer person in my own way, to start building a community.

II.

I'm waiting on a stoop outside my building for Rashid and Salwa to pick me up. It's the kind of summer day that is both cool and cloudless—perfect for the wedding we're attending two hours upstate from the city, of a mutual friend of ours from the mosque. *How are you guys getting there?* I had texted them the day before, after mapping out a route involving two buses, a train, and a cab.

We borrowed a car from my dad! Rashid had written back. *We'll give you a ride.*

Are you sure? I'm in Manhattan, and I know you Brooklyn people don't like coming into my borough on weekends.

Yes! We gotchu!

But I don't mind taking public transport, I replied. *Picking me up will add a lot of time to your trip.*

Cool, we can spend it together. Stop being so self-reliant! We would never let our Lamya take the train while we have a car.

Their tenderness had made me tear up. That's when I decided to tell them I'm queer.

Even now, as I sit on the stoop, my eyes get watery thinking about their text. But my earlier resolve to come out has dissipated, replaced by fear. *It'll be okay, Rashid and Salwa are your friends,* I say to myself over and over. *What's the worst that could happen?* But my leg won't stop shaking, I'm sweating straight through my one fancy kurta, and even the smell of cumin and paprika drifting from the shawarma cart on the corner can't calm me down. I make myself take a deep breath. *It's not a big deal.*

But it feels like a big deal. Rashid and Salwa are the first people from my mosque whom I've considered telling I'm queer, and the idea terrifies me, makes me want to cover myself with a heavy blanket. I'm scared partly because my mosque community is so close-knit: everyone seems to know someone who knows someone who knows my uncle upstate, and gossip travels at the speed of sound. I'm scared that somehow everyone at my mosque will find out. And I'm scared of the rampant homophobia in my mosque—not because it's unique to Muslims, but because the homophobia of Muslims feels like more of a betrayal. These people who will be there with me through death prayers and financial woes and the institutional racism of this country, who will stand next to me through long prayers in Ramadan. These people who are my people. Who know what it's like to be shunned for Muslimness but can't extend that empathy to queerness. It's less heartbreaking that they don't know.

Rashid and Salwa are the most Muslim of my friends, and they're special to me because of how they carry their Muslimness: as a lens for social justice, a force for building community, something to be constantly putting effort into and learning about. They take their Islam very seriously, not just in terms of ritual but also in terms of spirituality and text and centuries of classical interpretation. Just last month, they invited me to a lecture on the fiqh of Zakah, and I never could have guessed how much I'd enjoyed learning the esoterica of the laws around giving charity. After the talk, Salwa had turned to me and asked, "Where to next?"

"It's late. I was going to go home and sleep, guys."

"No way! Come with us to our favorite restaurant!"

Their favorite restaurant turned out to be a no-frills deli around the corner, where the Bangladeshi uncle at the cash register had salaamed with pleasure when they walked in. We ordered chai—two strong cups for them, none for my caffeine-sensitive self—and the uncle insisted we eat some of the fresh pakoras that had just come hot out of the frying pan. Rashid, Salwa, and I had talked for hours in that deli about the lecture, our favorite organizations to donate to, how best to give charity as financially insecure twentysome-things living in one of the most expensive cities in the United States. I had wheedled them into showing me their "giving spreadsheet"—a breakdown of their yearly donation budget and how to allocate it—and had been so impressed that I had gone home and made one for myself.

Being around Rashid and Salwa has never failed to make me a better person, a better Muslim. But also, it's been hard watching them grapple with gayness for the two years we've been friends. In one of our first conversations, we had been talking about issues that the Muslim community faces when one of them had bemoaned "the homosexual agenda." I remember exactly the cross streets we were walking on when they said that; I remember that another friend of ours had argued with them; and I remember how my ears started ringing and I didn't hear anything they said for the next few city blocks. Other times, they spoke about disagreeing with a mutual friend who "decided" to be gay, or their skepticism for a friend's "rationale" for dating a woman.

Which makes them sound like the worst possible candidates to come out to, or even be friends with—except. I met them when I was new to the city and needed Muslim friends, so I stuck around for longer than I normally would have, and I'm glad I did. Rashid and Salwa have since made openly gay friends in grad school, expanded their under-standing of queerness, and now, it feels unthinkable that they'd say—or even think—some of the things they used to. But I want them to continue to confront their own homophobia, to grow. I know that they love me and I'm sure that my coming out will force them to rethink some of their prejudices and preconceptions. I've come close to telling them a few times, but there's always something I latch on to as an excuse: that another friend is joining us. Or that they're late when we meet up so they're all frazzled from being late and I'm angry that they're late, so it's definitely not a good time to tell them. Or I'm having a hard day, or I'll just tell them next time, or I'm just not ready yet.

But today is the day, I've decided. And to fully commit to my decision, I tried a new strategy: earlier this morning, I texted them: *Can't wait to see you both in a few! Remind me I have something to tell you.* Now I can't not tell them. It's practically done.

Hence the nerves, hence the leg that won't stop jiggling, the pits that won't stop sweating. But then their car rounds the corner and they look so pretty dressed up in all their finery and they're rolling down their windows and waving and falling out of the car in their enthusiasm to see me and I breathe, I breathe. *It's okay. They're your friends and they love you,* I tell myself. And climb in.

After the obligatory *hi how are you how was your week?* Salwa interrupts my stream of questions about the two of them, my attempt to deflect the conversation away from myself. She turns around from the front seat of the car and looks at me. "What did you want to tell us?" she says.

"Oh." I say, caught. But the words come easier than I'd anticipated. "Guys. I wanted to tell you that I'm gay."

"Whoa! I did not see that coming," Salwa says. I see the

quick glance she exchanges with Rashid, and I'm not sure what transpires between them in that instant, but the next thing she says is completely different in tone.

"I'm so happy for you!"

In an instant, all my trepidation melts away and I instantly feel lighter. "I'm sorry it's taken so long for me to tell you guys."

"Sorry not needed at all," Rashid says. "You're allowed to tell people on your own timeline."

"Are you dating someone?"

"Do other people in the community know?"

And so forth. They ask a whole bunch of questions about what it's been like, neutral questions at first, nothing about haram and halal. And then the questions become progressively more caring. They want to know who's been supportive and who hasn't. They ask if there's any queer programming at the Islamic center, they're shocked that there's none and are happy to listen to me rant. It's kind of nice actually, the normalcy of the questions and the ways in which our friendship and rapport feel unchanged. And then Rashid stops midway through a question he's asking and suddenly turns serious.

"Listen. I'm prone to saying ignorant things about queerness sometimes. Please don't let it slide. Please tell me if I ever do that. Please hold me accountable."

Salwa nods, too. It is so beautiful, this moment. It makes me want to cry.

And that moment of genuine introspection from my friends is not their last. Over time, more emerge. They notice that there's a queer Muslim who's new in their program at school and ask what the best ways are to support her. One of their roommates on a summer trip is gay and they ask how to make sure he's comfortable. I get a call one day from both of them on speakerphone, asking me how to use "they" pronouns.

These questions never fail to make my day. And remind me that it was the right decision to tell them I'm gay.

III.

You. You're forty years old when you receive the wahi one ordinary night and suddenly your life becomes extraordinary. Suddenly, you're al-Mustafa, the chosen one. Suddenly you're a nabi, an apostle from God; a rasool, a prophet with a mission and a message—to believe in God, one God, to do good, to call others to do good. And that message must be shared.

You share the message in secret at first. You're careful about telling only those whom you trust: your wife, Khadijah, of course, who believes you. And then your best friend, your cousin, your daughters, your adopted son, all of whom believe you, all of whom convert to Islam. Slowly, you invite others into this circle of trust. You build a small following, a small community.

One day, a man named Umar finds out about you. His sister is among the early converts, and he is angry, he has decided he wants to kill you, but first he wants to kill his sister. He marches out of his house with his sword unsheathed, stalking the streets and roaring in displeasure. He finds his sister at her house, reading some verses that have recently been revealed to you through the wahi. "Show me these verses," Umar demands, and his sister reads them to him.

> *Ta Ha*
> *We have not revealed [these verses] to cause you*
> *distress*
> *But as a reminder [to do good] for those in awe [of*
> *God]*
> *A revelation from the One Who created the land and*
> *the skies*
> *[From God, Who is] the Most Merciful . . . (20:1–5)*

Umar is taken aback. He is known far and wide as someone who is principled and just, who knows right from wrong instinctively, and this is not what he was expecting from these verses. "Take me to Muhammad," he orders his sister.

You. You see Umar coming through the window, sword still unsheathed by his side. Are you afraid? Do you want to run and hide? Or do you practice what you'll say? Do you talk to yourself, tell yourself it'll be okay?

Umar walks in through the door that day and says he believes in God, your God.

I can imagine your elation, your relief, because I feel it, too. It's that glorious feeling that comes from inviting someone into your world.

IV.

My friend invites me to breakfast at her new job in a fancy tech office. There's a free buffet every day, she tells me, hot food *and* six different types of cereal *and* fresh pineapple. My friend knows my weaknesses very well: it's been three long years since my last breakfast buffet in college, my favorite meal, my favorite kind of buffet. Her targeted advertising is extremely effective, and I agree to meet up with her at seven in the morning, before work.

It's been at least a year since my friend and I have seen each other, even though we used to see each other all the time. We've known each other for a while, since college in fact, where we met as freshmen at a Muslim Students Association meeting and bonded instantly over being the only two hijabis in our class. We've been through a lot together since then: in-fighting within the MSA board, organic chemistry finals, brutal, snowy winters. We both moved to New York after college and continued to be there for each other: through housing drama, job searches, and nasty friend circle politics. She's my favorite person to talk to about religion. She grew up in a Muslim household very similar to my own in terms of practice, and she understands my attachment to faith because she is similarly attached. I'm constantly inspired by the way she practices Islam, both thoughtfully and unapologetically. She prays everywhere: parks, the beach, the back room of a bar at a friend's birthday, once even at Flushing Meadows when we were watching the men's U.S. Open semifinals. She's incredibly well

read about Islam and is similarly angry at patriarchy; conversations with her about fiqh and justice always leave my
faith in faith renewed. And, best of all, she gives great hijab-
pinning advice and has an extensive collection of borrow-
able scarves. She's one of my favorite people, this friend.

This year is the longest we've gone without seeing each
other. For lots of small reasons: she just started this new job
and got busy with work; I've been putting in late nights
working on my qualifying exams for graduate school; she
moved to an outer borough and can't hang out on weekends;
I don't do mornings, her preferred time to hang out. But
there's a big reason, too. She doesn't know that I'm queer.

It's not like I'm hiding that I'm gay from this friend, it's
not that I don't want to tell her. It's just that the more I've
grown into my queerness, the less I want to come out to
straight people. It's been a few years since my early experiences coming out, two years since I came out to Billy's
mom, and a few months since I came out to my friends from
the mosque. But every telling still feels like a momentous
act of vulnerability, a venture into the unknown. How will
the person react? What if they're homophobic? What if
they're Islamophobic? Will they be supportive? I've learned
to reframe telling people as inviting in, instead of coming
out—inviting into a place of trust, a space for building—
and it feels like a waste of emotional energy to tell straight
people whom I don't expect to understand my queerness,
don't intend to count on for advice or support in this area.

But what I've been noticing about people I haven't invited into my queerness is that it introduces a barrier be-

tween us. What do I talk to these people about? How do I share feelings and intimacies without revealing this huge part of myself? Who am I without this queerness that now pervades my life, my politics, my everything? It's so strange not to share this, so I've stopped putting in the effort to hang out with most of the straight people in my life, apart from the friends from my mosque. Consequently, a lot of my older friendships have started to slowly die out.

This friend, however, is persistent. Even though we haven't been able see each other in a while, she texts me consistently and ramps it up once she's settled in at her new job. She wants us to hang out, wants us to be in each other's lives, and her dedication is contagious. It makes me want all of those things, too, and reminds me that she's one of my favorite people, that I want to make an effort with her, want people in my life who have known me for a long time. So I wake up at six in the morning—an hour I wasn't sure even existed. I put on an outfit appropriate for a tech office, instead of the running tights I wear most days to work. Then I trudge to my least favorite place in this city: midtown.

My friend starts filling me in on all the gossip that's going on in her life even before we're out of the elevator. She laughs as my eyes widen at the decadent breakfast spread, sneaks me a Tupperware box under the table that she's brought so that I can take home an extra bagel. I can't talk for the first half hour because I'm so busy stuffing myself full of food: pancakes and hash browns and yogurt and granola and grapefruit and orange juice—so many of my favorite foods and, best of all, free. While I eat, she tells me how her three sisters are doing, how much she loves having a car now that she lives in a neighborhood with parking, that her parents are thinking of moving to the East Coast.

I'm on my second helping when my friend tells me that she wants to get married. Now that she has a stable job, her next endeavor is to put serious effort into this whole finding a guy and getting married thing. I'm not surprised, but I'm definitely curious about how she's navigating halal dating. Very poorly, she says. She complains about how hard it all is. Her parents have been setting her up with some very mediocre men, and Minder—the Muslim Tinder app that everyone seems to be using—has led to some very awkward situations. I laugh as she describes a dinner date where the guy insisted on bringing his sister as a chaperone; a coffee date with a guy who insisted on meeting at a Starbucks inside a Target store; a date where the guy handed her a printout of his résumé.

"What about you?" she says finally, when my second plate is nearly empty. "Are there any guys you're interested in?"

I take a deep breath. It's now or never. I've seen for the past year how difficult it is to maintain our friendship without sharing this part of me, and if I lie now, I won't be able to undo it easily. I gather every ounce of courage I possess.

"I've actually been meaning to tell you something."

"What's going on?"

Embarrassingly, I start shaking with nerves.

"Whatever it is, I support you," she says into the silence that I can't seem to break.

Again, the brink, followed by free fall. "I'm queer."

"Oh, cool," she says, like it's no big deal, and I'm still shaking, but immediately I feel better, especially when she launches into a story about another guy she went on a few dates with. I've tuned out for a bit to calm myself down, but I tune back in when she says that she told him it wouldn't work out between them because he'd told her he was bi-sexual.

"Wait, what?" I say.

"I just couldn't figure out why he needed to tell me he's bi. It seemed like such an unnecessary confession."

I'm confused. "Really? You can't think of any reason why a man you're interested in getting to know for marriage would tell you beforehand that he's bisexual?"

"I mean, yeah, I can think of a few reasons, but I couldn't figure out why he *needed* to tell me. If we got married, it wouldn't be relevant because he'd be with a woman. So why tell me in the first place?"

"Because it's important for him not to keep secrets from a potential partner? I don't get why this was a big deal to you—I just told you that I was gay and you were fine?"

"Yeah, but that's different. It's a private thing for you, you don't tell people for the sake of telling people. You don't go around shouting it from the mountains. You're not gay like *that*."

Pleasure and relief wash over me. I told her that I'm gay and she still likes me. She likes the private way that I'm gay. She wants to stay friends with me. Her acceptance makes me feel extra gregarious. At the end of our breakfast date, I tell my friend that we should do this more often, we should get breakfast together every week. I tell her that we should go to yoga, too, some mornings, that I'll come out to her new place to visit her, that we should start a halaqa together, that I miss her, anything and everything to reiterate her assessment that I'm not gay like *that*.

It is not until later that evening when I'm crawling into bed that the relief subsides and what fills me instead is horror. I can't believe I let her get away with what she said. What does she even mean I'm not gay like *that*? Being queer is a private thing for me because I don't feel safe telling people; specifically, I don't feel safe telling straight people. I'm not shouting it from the mountains because we live in an intensely homophobic world. What silence, what shame, does she want from me in exchange for her friendship, her acceptance? And that is when disgust takes over and suffuses through my body, disgust at myself and anger at myself. For who I became in that moment this morning, in this moment of wanting her to like me. For playing the part of the good queer, the private queer, the nondisruptive queer who doesn't challenge the status quo, doesn't threaten the dominant paradigm. I fall asleep hating myself.

V.

You. God sends you the wahi one ordinary night, and then the wahi keeps coming. Unpredictably at first; there are days swollen with revelation and weeks without. And then suddenly, one day, you receive the revelation that you must have

known was coming. God says it's time to publicly proclaim
the message. To take this step that will change everything.

Does it feel to you like a momentous act of vulnerability,
this venture into the unknown? Are you nervous about how
people will react? Do you shake? None of the stories in the
seerah answer my questions, none of them tell me how you
felt. In the stories, you tell people with no hesitation, no
second thoughts. You run up a mountain and call on the
people below. You tell them that you have something to say.
A crowd gathers below you. You are, after all, al-ameen—the
trustworthy. You're their cousin, their nephew, their friend,
you're known to them and they want to hear what you have
to say.

"Would you believe me if I told you there was an army
behind this mountain?" you ask.

"Yes, we would," the crowd replies. "You are not a liar."

You tell them to believe what you're saying, that you are
a messenger from God. You tell them about the wahi. That
God has been revealing to you the Quran. In it are instructions. On how to worship, how to pray and fast and take
care of orphans, how to live justly, how to be. You ask them
to believe you. You ask them to follow Islam. When you are
done speaking, there is silence.

"May you be ruined," a voice rings out. It is your uncle,
the brother of your father. He is an influential figure in your
city, and he calls loudly and angrily for an end to this mad-
ness. It is enough to scare everyone. The crowd disperses.

Later, a different uncle, your favorite, summons you to
his home. He is the head of your tribe and bound by the
laws of society to protect you. He asks you if what he's heard

is true, if you've been telling everyone you're a prophet, if you've been converting people to Islam.

"Why are you doing this?" he asks. "Can't you do all of this in secret? Why shout it from the tops of the mountains? What is this need to tell everyone?"

If you're not disruptive, he says, he can protect you. "Just keep it to yourself, just preach in private."

You. You answer with a firm no. No, thank you. You tell your uncle that you don't need his protection. God will protect you. That even if you were given the sun in your left hand and the moon in your right hand, you would never give up what God has asked you to do. You're not ashamed.

I am not that brave. I am ashamed—not about my queerness, but for not standing up to my friend. I don't confront her directly, but I stop hanging out with her after that breakfast. Something shifts between us that neither of us is willing to acknowledge. We still text occasionally, but our communication slowly fizzles until it dies out altogether. It's not perfect or graceful, but it is a tiny step toward changing how I interact with the people in my life, what I accept in my friendships, whom I surround myself with. It's a beginning toward inventing myself anew.

VI.

A new friend invites me to her birthday. *It'll be super casual,* she texts, *brunch on Sunday / just a bunch of queers / bring something to share—maybe chips and hummus?* I have never been able to pull off the whole casual thing, but I put significant effort into sounding chill in my text back: *Sounds great / I'll be there.* On the inside, though, I'm jumping up and down and embarrassingly ecstatic. A queer birthday potluck brunch? I've made it.

I've been friend-chasing this person for a few weeks now—and not just her. I've been friend-chasing her entire crew. I met them all a few months ago at a protest, friends of Billy's friends. I was immediately intrigued: they were visibly and enthusiastically queer, as well as political, angry, and invested in changing the world. It was hard not to want to be in their orbit. I was smitten.

They're not perfect people, this group of friends—we got dinner after the protest, and as the evening progressed, it became clear that they were flawed and messy and that there were tensions within the group. But despite this, there was an ease to them, an ease in the way they were with each other. They were comfortable in their own skin: expressing joy and making mistakes and living, just living. I wanted that ease so badly—both with myself and with others. Being around this new crew made me feel hungry for examples of how to live my queerness, how to feel less alone.

So I friend-chased. Added everyone in the crew on social media and hit like on their posts. Went to spoken-word shows they were performing at, waved to them from across the room at lectures and events; and on days when I was feeling bold, even sat next to them. Asked for their phone numbers and invited them to get coffee. I put in the effort and it started working; slowly, I built friendships with everyone individually, and slowly, I started infiltrating their friend group.

And now, this queer birthday brunch is the first time since the protest that I've gotten an invite to hang out with them as a crew, and I'm nervous. It feels kind of like an audition, a chance to wow them as a group. I decide to embrace my nervousness fully: I always feel better being well prepared for exams. So I go all out: I taste test four different kinds of Boycott, Divestment, Sanctions–compliant hummus before settling on Whole Foods jalapeño. Go to three different stores until I find my favorite brand of multigrain chips. Pick out my most super casual queer outfit to wear: a gray button-down and boy jeans and a skull print hijab. Show up a little early to the brunch but lean against a wall around the corner and read my book so I can be exactly, precisely twenty minutes late. I am determined to rock this audition.

But I shouldn't have worried. As soon as I enter my new friend's sunny, cozy, plant-filled apartment, she greets me warmly, and the few people who are already there jump up to say hello before I'm fully inside the door. "I didn't know you were coming! I'm so glad you're here!" says one of the queer femmes whom I've been very intimidated by, and who has previously been hard to read. "It's been so fun getting to know you the past few weeks," says one of the nonbinary cuties. My jalapeño hummus is a huge hit—three people come up to me during the course of the afternoon and tell me that it's their favorite flavor, and we commiserate over how hard it is to find good hummus. Everyone wants to know my opinion on the new Zadie Smith book that I posted about on Facebook. It feels like these people are my real friends. *Don't get too used to this, Lamya. Don't fuck this up,* a tiny voice in my head says. But I'm having so much fun that I manage to drown it out.

Toward the end of the afternoon, when the drop-ins and coworkers and casual acquaintances have left, Adam comes to find me, with his partner in tow. I've only really started to connect with Adam over the last week or so, but he's currently my favorite out of everyone in the crew. I'm grazing at the brunch table, a little mortified at being caught eating my favorite bits—the crumbs and burned cheese at the bottoms of the pans—but Adam finds it hilarious.

"See, this is why I really wanted you to meet my partner," he says. "I think you'll really get along."

"Save me some of that leftover salad dressing to drink," the partner says.

"That's my favorite, too!" I exclaim.

Adam's partner and I are fifteen minutes deep into a snarky conversation about weird but delicious foods when Adam drifts away and joins the group that's congregated around the TV watching YouTube videos of Lady Gaga. I feel content, here at this table at this party, talking and eating with this person I'm getting to know.

"You know, I'm really glad we were introduced," Adam's partner says.

"Me, too!"

"For real, though. Adam won't stop talking about how cool you are, and I'm really glad we're getting to know each other. I would otherwise have studiously avoided the religious Muslim in the room."

He's not being serious, is he? He said that to mock the stereotypes embedded in this situation, right, this conversation between a white gay man and a hijabi? I pause for a beat, waiting for a laugh or a *just kidding* that doesn't come. His face is earnest. Oh, God, he's being entirely, absolutely earnest.

It hits me then that I am the only one in the room: the only practicing person of faith, the only hijabi, the only visible Muslim, even in this multiracial group of political queers who pride themselves on nonnormativity. It's not something I'm unused to, this whole being the only visibly different person in the room thing, this whole having to play the stereotype crusher, the not-oppressed, the receptacle of unintentional racism. But it hits me hard, the constancy of the burden that I carry, and how different this burden feels today. Even to this crew, I have to prove myself. *You all know I'm queer, but I still have to play the cool hijabi*, I think, my gaze shifting from Adam's partner to the rest of the group, now watching the music video for "Bad Romance" for the second time. *The not-too-religious hijabi, the hijabi who can rock it with the alternative crowd, who won't judge you, who will be accepting and tolerant, the Good Muslim.* I'm in full-on silent rant mode now. *Unlike those Bad Muslims, the religious ones, the ones who are inconvenient in their practice, the ones you have to pause for as they break their fasts, the ones who have to step out to pray. The marginalized ones you would fight for, organize for, protest for, but would never be friends with, who you would studiously avoid at a brunch. I'm the cool hijabi only because you're projecting your xenophobic narrow-mindedness, your lack of imagination about Muslims onto me. You're still projecting them. Your prejudices are still in the room.*

Adam's partner clears his throat and I realize I've turned glassy-eyed with private rage while he's been standing there, waiting a little too long for me to respond. So in an effort to dispel the awkwardness of the situation, I force out a laugh, suppress my anger, and put myself on autopilot. I know all too well how to play the part of the Good Muslim. Because the embarrassing truth is, I still want to be friends with him, with this crew. I change the subject and ask him questions about his family and his job. When it turns out we work only a few blocks from each other, I tell him we should get coffee sometime and we exchange phone numbers. I become even more gregarious and feel a rush of pleasure when he recip-rocates; from the outside, we must look like we're in a com-mercial about instant best friendship. But from a corner of my brain, my anger whispers: *See? I can be who you want me to be. I can be cool. I can hang with you all.*

After a half hour or so, I say my goodbyes to protests of *but why* and *stay a little longer, we're going to order pizza,* and *what do you have to do on a Sunday anyway?* When I get home, I go straight to my bed and lie down. I breathe. And then begin to cry. For how terrible I feel, how disgusting. For playing, yet again, this part that feels so false and dis-honest and unfair, this part that only exists because of its corollary, this part that comes at the cost of others.

VII.

You. Your world is different with the wahi in your life, with your public announcement to the world about Islam. You're punished heavily by the community for telling people you're a prophet, for calling people to good. And it's not just the people in power who are punishing you, it's also your family, your tribe, those who are supposed to protect you, and it's not just you who are being punished, it's also your followers. You bear the punishment for years. It takes different forms. Always some sort of poverty: no one will employ you, no one will buy from you. For three years, there's an organized boycott of the early Muslims: no one will talk to or trade with or marry your followers, you're forcibly moved to an area on the outskirts of the city, and you're left hungry and downtrodden. And then there's the physical abuse: one day while you are praying at the Kaaba, someone dumps the entrails of a camel onto your back. Your neighbor throws garbage in front of your door daily. Your followers are tortured and killed for believing in Islam. You've all become pariahs. And you bear it, but it wears on you.

One day, out of the blue and in the midst of this despair, you're summoned to a meeting by the leaders of your tribe. They want to talk to you, want to hear what you have to say, and they have a proposal. You must have been overjoyed, no? You must have been elated. It's everything you've been waiting for: a chance, an audition. An audience with the most powerful people in your city; they're taking you seriously and giving you an opportunity to present your message. If you could get through to even one of them, you'll be

HIJAB BUTCH BLUES   143

saved from the misery that you and your followers have sunk
into, you'll be respectable, you'll have some clout. Did you
prepare arduously for this meeting? Did you pick out your
best clothes, arrive early? Did you let yourself dream of how
different your life would be after this meeting? Did you let
yourself feel hope and elation?

When you arrive at the meeting, it's clear from the beginning that it's not quite what you expected it to be. The
leaders are not interested in listening to you, your message,
or how hard it's been for your followers. They've invited you
here with a specific agenda: to buy you out. They've pooled
their resources, drawn up all their influence and authority.
"What will it take?" they ask you. "What will it take for you
to abandon this Islam thing, this religion that's threatening
our customs and dividing families. What will it take to give
up this small following you have, of the marginalized, the
poor, the hungry?" Name your price, they tell you, and they
will match it. "Do you want money? Do you want power or
influence or a title? A son to adopt? Whatever it will take,
just name it."

You're not interested. You're still trying to convince the
leaders to listen to you, trying to salvage this conversation
from going nowhere. In the middle of this conversation with
the most powerful men in your city, a man approaches you,
interrupts, and tries to get your attention. His name is Abdul-
lah, meaning "servant of God," and he is poor and blind. He
is one of your followers. He wants to learn Quran, wants
you to teach him. The leaders sneer and look away in disgust. And you. You frown.

You frown and you turn away. You go back to this conver-

sation you're embroiled in, continue trying to convince
these leaders, these rich men, these men of power. Is it because you want them to know you're one of the cool ones?
The ones who are religious but not like *that*? The reasonable
ones? The ones who it's worth talking to, the normative
ones, the ones they would never studiously ignore at a
brunch? Do you want them to like you? Do you, too, feel a
rush of pleasure that they continue talking to you, that they
approve of you turning away this poor, blind follower of
yours, so that you continue to focus your attention on them?

After a while, it's clear that the leaders are not going to
listen to you and you refuse their offers. You're not doing
this for money or power, you're preaching Islam because
you believe in its power to change society, you believe in the
power of God to change society, you believe in justice, and
you refuse to be bought. But that frown. Your frown.

God sees that frown. God sees everything: what's in
your heart, what's in your mind, what you intended, and
your little and big mistakes. God sees the inadvertent consequences of your frown, the hierarchies that it establishes,
the way it plays to power. And God sees why you frowned:
how badly you wanted the leaders to listen, how badly you
want to be seen and respected. Not for yourself but for
God. For Their religion, and for the followers of Their religion, to lift the Muslims out of misery.

But God reprimands you for that frown. God sends you
a wahi, a chapter of the Quran dedicated to this reprimand:
Surah 'Abasa, meaning "He frowned." *You shouldn't have
done that*, the surah says. The chapter is about how God

guides whom They will and leads astray whom They will.
You can't make someone listen to you, you can't make someone respect you. You can only respect yourself, and the best
way to do that is to enact justice, to live love. For the poor,
the blind, the marginalized, those on the outskirts of society, those people who are not in power, those people who
are your people, those whom you come from, those who are
yours. It's difficult to read this surah, hard to not be mortified on your behalf, Muhammad, but God speaks to you in
this surah.

And God speaks to me, too, through this surah. *Don't lose
yourself. Don't pander to those with influence, with access to
power. Don't try so hard with the cool kids, not at the cost of
denigrating your people, not at the cost of entrenching stereotypes, not at the cost of hating yourself. Don't expect others to
alleviate your problems, your loneliness. Because they can't,
only God can do that, and God will. God will.*

VIII.

Join us for a performance of the "Coming Out Muslim" play,
the email reads. *LGBTQ+ Muslim meetup to follow for people who hold those identities, no allies please.* I get this message on an activist email group a few months after the queer
birthday brunch, a few months during which I've been trying and failing to find queer Muslims in the city. This email

with its intentional wording, its nod to privacy and consideration of safety, feels like a sign. It feels like God is telling me to go.

But still, I'm scared. The venue is four blocks away from my mosque. What if someone sees me going in? My cousin has just moved to the city for grad school; what if someone she knows is there? What if no one likes me? What if I'm not legible as queer?

"Just go!" Billy tells me. He offers to walk me into the event, promises me that I can leave if I recognize anyone in there, that he'll pick me up after if I need a decoy. I am touched anew at his kindness but decline his help. This feels like something I need to do alone.

But as soon as I walk in through the door for the meetup, it's clear that I'm not alone. The room is in the back of the theater and is small and sparsely lit, but in it are the most beautiful people I've ever seen, of varying genders and hairstyles and hijab styles, of varying ages, of varying shades of Black and brown. The space has been set up so thoughtfully, with food in the back and in the front, and a person at the door whose job it is to welcome new folks. She gives me a sticker for my pronouns and directs me to a group of people who are standing around talking. The group greets me like a long-lost friend. They're talking about the play, telling their own "coming-out" and "not-coming-out" stories, and it's easy to tell a few stories of my own, to not have to explain my queerness and Muslimness. It's so easy to just be.

I'm in bliss, drifting between the different groups of people and the snack table, when I see a new friend take the mic. Manal, whom I met a few minutes ago and instantly bonded with over our mutual love of well-labeled food and similar Muslim upbringings, makes an announcement.

"A few of us are going to pray Maghrib now," she says. "Folks are invited to join us or not, whatever works for you!"

The group separates, and we shuffle into parallel lines. I move toward the back expecting to join the women like I do at my mosque, when I notice that folks aren't segregating by gender, that people of all genders are praying side by side, shoulder to shoulder, equal in the eyes of God. It has never even occurred to me that I could pray this way, and I feel something bordering on euphoria as I make my way to the front line behind the imam—a row in which I've never prayed before. I even volunteer to say the Iqama.

After the prayer, folks are starting to leave when someone comes in late, a person in a plaid shirt and funky blue glasses, sporting the classic queer haircut—short on the sides and long and curly on top—and so much butch swagger that the energy in the room changes. My jaw drops. They're an aspirational version of me, and I find myself wondering if they're an illusion, someone I manifested into appearing at this gathering that feels like a window into jannah. But they're greeted with cheers of *Hi, Zu!* and hugs, and it's clear that they're very real and very loved. I get suddenly shy and drop back to the peripheries.

Zu does the rounds as I scramble to take down names and numbers before people leave, desperate to connect, desperate to re-create this magic again. Suddenly, they're beside me, talking to me.

"Don't worry about getting everyone's contact info," Zu says. "We meet up a lot. I'll loop you in."

"Thanks," I say, embarrassingly nervous for them to like me, cautiously ecstatic that they're seeing me as part of the community already. I'm worried I'm sweating through my one nice button-down.

I take a deep breath and decide to be vulnerable. "I feel like I've been looking my whole life for this community."

"Well, get ready to be folded in," Zu says. "There's a lot we have coming up. A bunch of us are going to the Dyke March next week, and someone was talking about starting a book club. Oh, and have you heard of the LGBTQ+ Muslim retreat?"

They laugh at how wide my eyes get. And then look me up and down, take in my skulls and flower hijab, my butch jeans and dyke boots.

"You remind me a lot of myself when I was younger. I wore hijab and was the president of the Muslim Students Association in college. Listen, if you ever have anything you want to talk about, hit me up."

All the axons in my brain are telling me to play it cool but I override them all. "Wait, are you saying you're willing to be my Queer Life Mentor?" I ask.

Zu laughs. "I guess that's what I just signed up for."

Finally, finally, I'm home.

IX.

You. You're forty years old when you receive the wahi and it changes your life and how you want to live it. You have some mishaps, make some mistakes along the way, but ultimately, there's this. God takes care of you. God is gentle, God is kind. They tell you to just be. Do you. Teach the Quran, spread the message, be grateful for the sustenance and the signs from God, be afraid of the Day of Judgment when everyone will be responsible for their own deeds.

And God guides you. To Islam first, then to a community of believers, then to a new city nearby, Madinah. The inhabitants welcome you with a song set to drums, a paean so reverent that they address you in second person, too respectful to even say your name. Finally, your community can put down roots and build anew. Finally, finally, you, too, are home.

ASIYAH

I.

My mother talks a lot about Asiyah.

She talks about Asiyah to me and my brother while we wait for my dad in the car. I am five years old and waiting is hard. We wait a lot, though, in those early years of what my mother calls our new life. We have just moved from the country where I was born, where we lived next door to my grandmother in a small bungalow with a yard, to a stuffy apartment in a wealthy Arab country where we don't know anyone. Here, in this new country, my mother can't drive and it's too hot to walk outside so we spend our days at home waiting for my dad. We wait for him to come home from work. We wait for him to change his clothes and do wudu and pray Maghrib. We wait for him to decide how tired he is, to find out what our evening will look like.

On days when my dad is not too tired, the four of us pile

into our car. It's exciting, getting to go somewhere other than school, seeing the city in the dark, lit up and alive. The stores, with their signs in flowery script, everything spilling out onto the sidewalks; the sprawling villas that we can only see the tops of, illuminated in purple and gold. And there's usually a treat to look forward to—ice cream or the swings at the park or balila by the sea—but first, before any of this, we run errands, which means waiting in the car while my dad goes into cramped stores filled with men. To my brother and me, this waiting feels interminable. My dad goes to the butcher, and we wait in the car. My dad gets a haircut and we wait in the car. My dad goes to the hardware store and we wait in the car, my mother in the front seat, and us bored and squabbling in the back.

My mother tells us stories while we wait for my dad in the car, sometimes fairy tales with morals; sometimes long, convoluted sagas that she spins on the spot; but mostly stories from the Quran. We love her stories; her voice is both spirited and soothing, and we're safe in the locked car from monsters and giants and the unknowns of the night. Whenever my brother and I are especially tired of waiting and our bickering escalates, my mother tells us the story of Asiyah.

"Once upon a time," she'll say. "A long, long time ago, there was a beautiful queen named Asiyah who was married to Pharaoh, the king of Egypt. Pharaoh was the most evil man that Allah had ever created. He was mean to everyone, but he was especially mean to his wife, Asiyah, who was the kindest, most patient woman on earth. Even when the pharaoh was rude to her, she was never rude to him. Even when he teased her and fought with her and called her names, she

wouldn't say anything. She would never grumble and com-
plain, and if she was in the car right now, she would tell you
how important it is to be kind and patient with each other,
and she would tell you that Allah promised her paradise
because of those two qualities. The end. Now can we practice being kind and patient with each other until Baba
comes back?"

My mother talks about Asiyah to the girls in our apartment
complex, at the Quran circle she runs every summer while
I'm in elementary school. Two hours every Wednesday
morning, we gather in each other's living rooms while she
talks about a different woman figure in Islam and I try not
to be mortified. The first lesson of the summer is always
about Asiyah, who my mother tells us is her favorite woman
in Islam—one of the four women who perfected their religion, and one of the first women who will enter paradise. A
true role model for us all.

My mother talks about Asiyah to my friends from middle school when she overhears us talking about being teased
for fasting in Ramadan. "Pharaoh tortured Asiyah because
she became Muslim," she tells us, while I try not to die of
embarrassment. "He took her out to the desert and cut off
her hair and humiliated her, and she still refused to de-
nounce Islam. Don't ever compromise your religion for
someone else."

My mother talks about Asiyah to her cousin, who calls
and cries so hard about not being able to get pregnant that
my brother and I, doing homework on the dining table, can

hear the sobs on the other end of the phone. My mother talks to her in hushed tones with lots of sympathetic noises in between. Tells her to do duaa, that maybe one day a baby Musa will float down the river and into her life. Tells her to be patient, that Allah will bless her with a child when she least expects it. Like Asiyah.

My mother talks about Asiyah with her friends, too, in the Islamic lectures for women that she goes to three mornings a week the year that I'm eleven. She makes me go with her when I'm sick or school is out. I protest every time. I'm old enough to stay at home alone and I even promise not to watch TV and it's so unfair because my brother doesn't have to go. But my mother is adamant, says that I have to go to the lectures because I'm a woman now, because I have to learn something new every day.

Not that there's anything new about these lectures: they're always at our neighbor's house, we always sit in a circle on starched white sheets spread on the ground, and the lecturer aunty always pinches my cheeks, demands that I recite whatever surah I've been memorizing in school. And at some point, regardless of what verses of the Quran are being discussed, someone invariably asks about Asiyah. *Is it true that Pharaoh hit her? That he stopped her from practicing her faith? That she stayed married to him even though she could have asked for a divorce?*

"Yes," the lecturer aunty will say. "Asiyah was married to the worst of men. He treated her terribly, humiliated her, and controlled everything that she did. But she had sabr throughout, the utmost form of patience. She bore every-thing with no complaints and stayed with him even when he tortured her. She prayed to Allah secretly and constantly. Do you know her duaa, ladies? Let's turn to surah sixty-six, verse eleven, and read it together. *My Lord, build for me near You a house in paradise and save me from Pharaoh and his deeds and save me from the wrongdoing people.* This is the kind of patience we need to have in our marriages. Divorce is the deed that's most hated to Allah. It splits up families and ruins children."

"*La hawla wa la quwwat illa billah,*" everyone in the cir-cle says. My mother hums in appreciation. We're always, somehow, talking about Asiyah.

II.

There were red flags about my cousin's fiancé even before she married him, the biggest and reddest of which was that he hadn't told her that he had been married before—twice. A few days before the nikah, my aunt found this out from a friend of a friend of a friend. The news spread quickly through our family. No one believed it at first—why did my cousin's fiancé not tell us, it couldn't be true, why did no one in the community tell us? When my aunt finally con-fronted her future son-in-law, his defense was that the mar-riages didn't count—the first marriage because it was called off before the walima celebration, and the second marriage because it was with a woman who wasn't Muslim. In retro-spect, this defense itself should have been a warning. There were lots of other red flags along the way: that my cousin would spend long hours trying to placate her fiancé on the phone, that he would get upset and threaten to call the wedding off, that he was unwilling to compromise on little things, like where they should go on their chaperoned dates and what color she should wear at the Mehendi event and how long they should get to know each other before they got married.

There were a lot of warnings, but my cousin got married anyway. Not because she was in love, but because she was desperate. She was visiting her sister in Cleveland and didn't want to go back; she was the only one of her siblings who wasn't living in the U.S., and even her parents were being sponsored for a green card through their son. My cousin's tourist visa gave her a six-month window before she had to leave, six months to figure out a way to stay. That wasn't a lot of time for her to find a husband, get married, and submit residency paperwork. And it's not as if the marriage offers were flowing in; she was dark-skinned and twenty-eight, at the cusp of being too old for the arranged marriage aunties. I was never close enough to this cousin to hear this directly from her, but she told her sister, who told my aunt, who told me that the wedding happened because my cousin was desperate. My cousin was convinced that this was the only way she would be able to live in the same country as the rest of her family. Besides, this man was attractive, had a financially stable job, prayed jumuah at the mosque every Friday, and most important, was American. So what if there were a few red flags? What could go wrong?

Turns out, a lot, which I hear from my mother on our

weekly phone calls. I refuse to tell my mother anything about my life in New York, I'm too scared that something about my queerness will slip. So she fills the silences in our conversations with stories that other people tell her instead: the time my cousin's husband yelled at her in front of everyone at a family wedding and then my cousin left crying and no one could find her for hours after the party ended; the time my cousin's husband got so angry at her that he took away her phone and everyone got scared because no one could get in touch with her for two weeks; and don't tell anyone, khuda ki qasam, Lamya, you really can't tell anyone this, but it seems like your cousin's husband might have a drinking problem.

One day my mother texts me, *it's imp pls call asap,* and adds a crying emoji. I'm in a graduate seminar and I rush out, stepping over people in my row, struggling to breathe as I imagine the horrible simultaneous deaths of everyone in my family. I say every protective duaa I know while the phone rings and jump when my mother finally picks up.

"Mama, is everything okay?"

"No. I have some very bad news for you. Where are you? Are you sitting down?"

I can hear in her voice that she's been crying. "Just tell me, Mama."

She pauses. I can hear her breathing in deeply, hesitating to say whatever it is, lest her saying it makes it more true.

"Your cousin asked her husband for a divorce."

I exhale for the first time since the beginning of the call. A relieved giggle slips out of me and I hold the phone away from my mouth so my mother can't hear. But quickly, this relief turns into anger.

"Wait, that's it? That's what you called me to say?"

"What do you mean that's it? Besharam. It's the first divorce in our family in generations. Everyone is so upset. I wanted you to hear about it from me."

I know, I know, I shouldn't argue with her, and I have the ethics of genetic engineering to get back to, but there's adrenaline coursing through me still, and I can't help myself.

"Mama, no offense, but this is good news. That man was horrible to her."

"*Astaghfirullah.* What is wrong with you? He wasn't that bad to her, and even if he was, that's not a reason to divorce him. Think of Asiyah. She lived with the worst man in the world and didn't divorce him."

"How can you say that? You're the one who's been telling me all these terrible stories about this man!"

"Yes, but you're only hearing one side of the story."

"There's no other side of the story! The things he's done have been so terrible that it doesn't matter what the other side of the story is."

"You don't know that. She must have provoked him. No one acts the way he did out of nowhere."

Anger pulsates through my veins, clouding my vision. I can't believe I stepped out of class for this, I can't believe I even tried to argue back. But I make myself breathe and count to five.

"I have to hang up now, Mama."

"Okay, but don't forget. These things don't happen out of nowhere. She must have done something to deserve this. She must have done something wrong."

III.

I come to the U.S. not out of love but out of desperation. I can't stay past high school in the Arab country where I grew up: universities are only open to citizens and there is no pathway to citizenship on the temporary worker expatriate visa that my family has been on for more than a decade. For the entire time I'm in high school, my parents worry. They're not emotionally or financially ready to move back to the country where we do have citizenship, where they could realistically afford to send me to college. We have no close family left there, so unless my parents moved with me, I'd have to live in a dorm or with distant relatives I barely know. And I'm worried, too: I haven't lived there since I was four, I don't speak Urdu well, and I don't want to go to medical school, which is the only tenable option open to women who want to study science.

But then, a series of miraculous things happen. I score highly on my SATs. I apply to a prestigious college in the U.S. on a whim and am accepted. The college costs more money than my family makes in a year, but I land a full tuition scholarship. My student visa is accepted, despite my wearing hijab to the interview, a decision that my father vehemently opposed. I am so sure something is going to go wrong that it doesn't sink in that I'm leaving until I'm on the plane. I get to leave. I get to go to college. I get to go to college in the U.S. and study whatever I want without bankrupting my family. I've gotten lucky. I was desperate, but I got this opportunity out of a difficult situation, and I got to take it. More miracles: the plane lands safely. I get through border security. My uncle is there to pick me up. Nothing goes wrong. I've moved to the U.S.

It takes me awhile to settle into this prestigious college. I make friends and do well in my classes and join clubs, but it still feels like I can't quite understand the culture of the place, like I'm always doing something wrong. The security guards always asking to see my ID are only the beginning. My concentration adviser, a middle-aged white woman, tells me the first time we meet that she's surprised my English is so good. She chides me about my class selection, says that I shouldn't have signed up for a foreign cultures course, that they could have waived the requirement for me because I'm obviously foreign. The TA for my four-hour organic chemistry lab yells at me when I ask if I can duck out to pray. One of my professors berates me in front of the whole class when I can't take an electroencephalogram reading because of my hijab, tells me that I need to stop using religion as an excuse for making everyone's life so difficult. It's hard not to feel like I'm always doing something wrong.

Two decades of life with a brother have left me pretty thick-skinned, but the incident that finally makes me cry happens one Tuesday afternoon when I take the bus to a museum downtown. I've been planning this outing for weeks: my first solo trip in the city, my first time at a museum, my first time seeing art in person. I'm organized and know exactly what I want to see in my two hours between classes: all the Impressionists and the Van Gogh and the new exhibit on Dadaism that I have spent hours reading about. I've gone through the museum's website and made a bulleted list in my journal of what's on each floor. I'm ready. I buy my discounted student ticket, pick up a map from the desk, and find a bench to sit on just inside the door. Armed with a highlighter and a pencil, I'm charting an optimal route through the exhibits when I feel someone standing behind me and turn around.

It's a cop.

He wants to speak to me, he says, tells me to come with him. Leads me to a sparse back room with security cameras and a green plastic chair. He's just going to ask me a few questions, he says. "What are you doing here? Where are you from? What are you doing at the museum? Are you here with someone else?" He wants to look at my map, wants to see my ID. He asks to look through my journal—a leather-bound notebook containing entries about my deepest thoughts and vulnerabilities, things that no one has ever read, things I've never said aloud. I hand my journal over and he flips through it, and suddenly I'm crying silently. I can't stop the tears from spilling out of my eyes. He looks up from reading the journal, sees me crying, and keeps reading. A few minutes later, he gives the journal back to me, says I can leave and to have a good visit at the museum. I've stopped crying by then, and I just want to go home, back to the relative safety of campus. But my pride won't let me do that. I wash my face in the bathroom and then reenter the museum, wandering halfheartedly through the rooms without really seeing anything until it's been long enough to justify the cost of the museum ticket and two bus tokens.

It's relentless, this feeling that I can't do anything right.

IV.

For years, I had been friends with one of our neighbors, but somewhere between her getting married and my leaving for college, she became my mother's friend instead. We had been close growing up; she lived in the building next door, and we'd work out together most evenings, either swimming in the pool of our apartment complex or running or, on rest days, we'd talk and play cards. Our parents were friends, too, so we would regularly end up at dinner parties together on weekends, often the only older unmarried girls at these boring gatherings segregated by gender and marital status. But then, just before I left for college, my friend got married. It was inevitable; all my childhood friends got married early. But the loss felt different with her. Being married meant that she spent evenings at home with her husband instead of with me and that she sat with the aunties at dinner parties. Then I left for the U.S., and between the logistical hurdles of us hanging out and the infrequency of my visits home from college and later grad school, she became my mother's friend instead. And they were real friends, too: they'd go to Islamic lectures and Tupperware parties together, and when her son was born, it was my mother who helped her out in the early weeks, my mother she'd call for advice. All of this felt at first like a betrayal, but over time, morphed into something else: a relief, maybe, that they had found each other and were able to give each other what they wanted from me, what I could not give them.

My mother would often share news of my neighbor in our phone calls, and in these stories were hints of how ter-

="4

ribly my friend's marriage was going. My mother wanted to take her to the new mall that opened near the beach, but they couldn't go because the neighbor's husband wouldn't allow it. The husband would call randomly to check up on her whenever she was out, and God help her if she didn't pick up the phone right away. Her husband once yelled at her so loudly that people in the building called the cops. "That's insane," I would say. "That's just marriage," my mother would say.

One morning, on my way to class, I call my mother and she says she can't talk right now, she's in a hurry, she and my dad are on their way out. I'm surprised; the time zone difference means that it's evening for them and it's a weeknight and my dad hates late nights out.

"We're going to an arbitration session," my mother says. I can hear her rifling through her purse, putting on her shoes.

"An arbitration session? For what? For whom?"

"For our neighbor. Did I not tell you about this? She wants a divorce and her husband doesn't. We offered to arbitrate so they can stay together. We're going to help them set some conditions for moving forward. Can you hurry up? We're running late," she yells to my dad as much into the phone as not.

"What? You're trying to get them back together? Why would you do that? He's horrible to her. That sounds like a terrible idea."

My mother pauses in her distracted preparation and I hear her take a deep breath. I brace myself for the rant I know is coming.

"You don't understand these things, Lamya," she says in

a tight, clipped voice. "This is just what marriage is like. What will she do if she leaves him? Where will she go? And she has a baby now, too; how will she support her child? You're being irrational. You know she can't legally stay in this country without a male guardian. She would have to go back to where she's from—and she has no one there. You don't understand how hard it would be. She just has to bear it. Think of how much Asiyah had to put up with when she was married to Pharaoh." She sighs. "You don't understand these things, Lamya. She has to have sabr, she has to be patient. Think of her future. Where will she go?"

V.

I'm always thinking about my future in the U.S.; I can't not. Because the country where my family lives is different from the country of my citizenship, which is different from the country where I went to college and am now in grad school, I'm constantly in a state of renewing visas and passports. I make color-coded spreadsheets listing my official documents arranged by dates of expiration, how long the documents will take to be renewed, and what needs to be renewed so other documents can be renewed. These spreadsheets are my best friends. The input trays of photocopiers, where it's so easy to forget originals of documents, are my enemies.

By the time I'm finishing graduate school, eleven years after first arriving in the U.S. for college, I'm four student visas in. Four times filling out extensive paperwork, four airplane trips to the one U.S. consulate in the country where my parents live. Four drives to the parking lot a mile away from the heavily armed visa application building, four bus rides on official consulate vehicles from the parking lot to the building. Four interminable waits in the visa lounge, shuttled from the eye scan to the fingerprint booth to the headshot. Four interviews in semiprivate cubicles, with steely white men behind Plexiglas who are either overly severe or overly friendly. Four times being asked questions designed to trip me up: *Can you tell me your parents' birthdays again? Have you ever been rejected for a visa before? You're not one of the ones we have to worry about, ha-ha-ha, right?* Four times facing the very real fear that this could all end, this life I'm beginning to build for myself in the U.S., this country that doesn't want me, after growing up in a country that didn't want me. It's terrifying that this life I'm living could all be over because of the suspicions of a midlevel visa employee, a missed expiration date, or a government policy change. Four times facing these fears head-on and decades of feeling them in my body, burning on low in the back of my mind. *This could all be taken away from you, Lamya. You could have to leave.*

While writing my graduate thesis, I find myself applying for jobs as well as a special visa extension that would allow me to work for a year in my field of study. The extension usually takes three months to process, but I don't know this until after I've submitted the application two months before my visa expires. I bank on being granted an extension in the thirty-day grace period before I would legally have to leave the country. I'm more worried about this extension than I am about finding a job. A few weeks after I submit the application, when I haven't heard back yet from the U.S. Citizenship and Immigration Services (USCIS) about scheduling a biometrics appointment, I start calling them every few days to ask if they have more information. "Applications processing is backed up at this time of the year," the person who answers the phone tells me. "Call after the normal processing time has elapsed." But I don't have that luxury: I would need to be out of the country by then and besides, I don't have health insurance in this in-between status, can't even go into work because my supervisor is too worried about the legality of letting me into the building.

And then, out of the blue, I get a call from the mailroom at the graduate housing building I've recently moved out of. They found some of my mail in a big, forgotten stash; it looks kind of official, can I come pick it up? I drop everything and bike over as quickly as I can, even though I know there's no point in hurrying. I know it's bad news, can't be anything but. And it is, of course. It's bad news. Two very official-looking letters from USCIS. I tear into them right there on the street, not caring that it's cold and windy, I just need to know. The first letter says that I need to submit a receipt to prove that I've paid one of the fees for the visa extension online. The second says that because it's been thirty days since I haven't submitted the receipt, my application is considered incomplete, my extension has not been granted, and my case is closed. Never mind that I had updated my mailing address before both letters were sent out, never mind that both letters still went to my previous address, never mind that I had gotten email confirmation that my mailing address had been changed in my file, never mind that I had called a few dozen times and talked to USCIS agents, that I had been told that there were no flags on my case, that I should just wait. I hadn't even considered the possibility that they would have contacted me at the wrong address. And now my extension has not been granted and my visa has expired and my case is closed.

I sit on the sidewalk, right there on the curb between two parked cars, and put my head down. I feel nothing. Not the letters in my hand, not my feet on the ground, the tightness in my throat, not sadness or anger or fear—none of the things I've been working on noticing in my body when I'm feeling anxious. Halfheartedly, I run through a few quick calculations. Five days since the last letter. Three days since my visa expired. Twenty-seven days until I have to leave the country. Around three thousand dollars to hire the lawyer that my friend gave me a number for, which is about three thousand dollars more than I have.

My phone rings. It's Zu, my Queer Life Mentor, who, in the two years since we met at the LGBTQ+ Muslim mixer, has taken their mentoring duties seriously and become a constant presence in my life. I was supposed to be having lunch with them right now but bailed so I could rush over to collect my mail. Zu has also spent a decade at the mercy of USCIS; they know what I'm going through right now and ask what the letters say without bothering with a greeting. I explain and they launch into a rant on my behalf, which is exactly what I need in this moment. I need their anger to snap me out of my numbness. When their tirade subsides, I say aloud, for the first time, the sentence that's been playing in the back of my mind for the past three months.

"That's it. I'm done with all of this. I'm leaving this country. I'm going back."

Zu is quiet for so long that I check my phone to make sure we haven't been disconnected.

Finally, they speak: "No."

"What do you mean, no? I've decided. I've had enough of this. I'm done."

"No, Lamya. You can't do this. You're queer and gender nonconforming. You're unmarried. You have no family in your country of citizenship and you speak shit Urdu. Where are you going to go? You're being irrational. This is just how the system works, you have to bear it. You'll have to appeal or reapply for a new visa or something; you'll figure it out. Think of your future. You can't just leave. What will you do? Where the hell will you go?"

VI.

A few days later, I get a call from a Seattle number that I don't know. I debate whether or not to pick up; I don't know anyone in Seattle whose number isn't already in my phone, I'm already in bed, reading, and it's taken me a few hours to de-stress from visa worries enough to consider sleeping. But something about the call is weird: my phone rings twice and stops, rings again until it goes to voice mail, and then rings once more, like the caller can't make up their mind. I pick up.

I'm surprised to hear the voice of one of my old friends from my mosque in New York on the other end. Surprised and excited and a little annoyed. We haven't talked in two years. "What do you mean you live in Seattle now?" I yell, not even trying to keep the annoyance out of my voice, even as I realize I'm partially taking out my visa stress on her. "I didn't even know you were leaving. How could you just leave and not tell me? That's not what friends do. I know you're always busy with work, but you haven't even responded to the last few texts I've sent and my emails to your account have bounced back. You know what, you suck at being a friend. I was genuinely afraid that you had died."

She's exactly how I remember her. Takes my tirade in stride, like she'd been expecting it. She's a lawyer and used to arguing back: she answers all of my complaints point by point, punctuates her responses with giggles, and calls me overly dramatic. I can almost hear her rolling her eyes at me through the phone. I'm relieved she's not dead. And it's nice to be talking to her like this again; there was a time when we saw each other almost every day, when we were indispensable parts of each other's lives. I settle into the conversation, get out of bed, and put in my headphones so I can fold laundry while I talk to her.

"I have something big to share," she says once she's finished her counterarguments.

"Bigger than moving across the country?"

"Bigger than moving across the country." She hesitates. "Well, kind of the reason why I moved across the country. Bilal and I got married."

Bilal. Her on-again, off-again secret boyfriend. Or rather "the person she was talking to about marriage," heaven forbid she or anyone in the mosque community call it what it is—a relationship, *astaghfirullah*. Bilal, who, in the six years that I had known my friend, in the six years of their varying degrees of togetherness, had never made time to meet her friends. Bilal who had once broken up with my friend on her birthday—in the middle of the not-date that he had planned for the two of them—because she had answered the phone when her aunt called. Bilal whom I subsequently referred to as "Babylal." The last I heard, Bilal had decided he could never marry my friend because of what he had deemed an irredeemable and unfixable character flaw: she didn't know how to speak Urdu. How would she ever communicate with his family? It was never going to work between them. The last I had heard, Bilal was out of the picture.

I offer my congratulations to my friend on her marriage; what else is one to do? She tells me they had a small wedding two summers ago with family only, that they moved to Seattle together for a fresh start, so fresh that she got a new phone number and email account. She loves being married, she says. She gets along well with Bilal's mom and sisters, but his dad has been harder to befriend. She's taking an Urdu class with an Indian aunty who lives in her building. It's always raining in Seattle, but it's an easy kind of rain, worth the dampness and the inconvenience because the summers are so beautiful, because the hiking is so great.

There's an edge to her voice, though, something out of the ordinary that I can't quite place. I weigh whether or not to ask the question that matters the most to me, especially when she's finally reaching out after two years, but maybe because it's been two years since I've heard from her, the question tumbles out of me.

"Are you happy?"

She pauses before she answers. "Mostly."

Something about her tone makes me sure there's something more there. So I stay silent. I wait.

And then she tells me the truth. Bilal has an easier time making new friends and has a crew from the mosque, but she's been struggling to connect with people out there; between the new number and the new email and the move across the country she's lost everyone she knew. Bilal is suspicious of everyone she meets, won't let her be friends with men or work colleagues. He gets angry when she dresses up to go outside but is upset when he gets home and she isn't dressed up. He wouldn't let her take a promotion at work because it involved a lot of traveling, and her company demoted her to a boring administrative job instead. He has the password to her phone and her email, goes through all her texts. She tells me she's calling from her work phone, and her voice is getting more and more frantic, as if she can't pause because if she does, she won't be able to say the rest.

"Yesterday he hit me," she says. "But he's not a bad man. He cried afterward because he was so ashamed that it left a bruise. He said that even though the Quran gave him permission, he promised that he'd never do it again."

My mouth is dry and I find myself holding the same towel I've been in the process of folding for five minutes. Somehow I gather myself and manage to tell her that this is not okay. It's not okay that he hit her, it's not okay that he's isolating her from her friends, it's not okay that he's controlling her life. The Quran doesn't give him permission to do any of this. I tell her these things, even though there is a lump in my throat that the words have to push past. Now she's crying on the phone and saying she hates it, she hates him, she wants to leave, but where will she go, she has no friends, she defied her family to marry him, where will she go? The sobs subside, but then panic enters her voice. "I have to hang up," she says. "Don't call me back at this number. I promise I'll call you back in a few days." I cry, too, when she hangs up. Ugly gulping sobs, wiping my tears on the clean towel I'm still holding.

My mother calls the next day, while I'm walking to work, and she finds a way to mention, as she does frequently, that I need to get married. Over the course of the night, my grief has metamorphized into anger and I end up telling my mother that I'm never getting married, that all of my friends are in abusive relationships, and suddenly I'm standing on a street corner, shaking and shouting at my mother, telling her about my friend whose husband hits her.

My mother waits for me to calm down before she speaks. "Think of Asiyah," she says. "Your friend can't have it worse than her, Lamya. Your friend is a lawyer with a great job. She makes a lot of money and can move anywhere she wants. She's a strong woman. It can't be as bad as she's making it seem, Lamya. If it was really that bad, she wouldn't stay. She would leave."

VII.

But, I stay.

I contact the department where I have interviewed for a job, tell them about my rejected visa situation, that they need to decide in the next few days if they're hiring me.

They call me the next day and offer me the job. And then they hustle: within six days, they manage to submit an expedited application for a work visa, which means that I can stay in the country while my application is processing. Another ten stressful days later, my work visa is accepted.

Then I have to leave the country to get a new visa stamp—in the eight days before my job starts. I fly out of JFK airport a bundle of nerves, willing myself not to catastrophize. I land in the country where I grew up and my parents still live, and my father drives me from the airport straight to the U.S. consulate to submit my application. It is a turnaround so tight that the visa interviewer gives me a stern talking-to. I nod and apologize, biting the inside of my cheek to keep from saying something stupid. He warns me that he can't guarantee that I'll get the visa in time. I call the consulate every day, hoping my being annoying will speed the process along. The morning of my late-night flight back to the States, the consulate calls me, says my visa is ready, and no, I can't pick it up, that's not standard protocol, they're going to FedEx it, it'll probably be delivered today. But evening comes and still no visa.

Four hours before my flight, my dad and I drive to the FedEx office. We cajole the man behind the counter to look through the next day's deliveries for my passport. He says he'll see what he can do and disappears into the back room. I pace back and forth in the fluorescent-lit office until my dad tells me to stop, to sit in a chair like a human being. An hour later, the man emerges from the back room with my passport, a shiny U.S. work visa on page fourteen. Three hours before my flight, the visa is finally in my hands, but I can't celebrate, I have no time. We rush home. I throw all my clothes into my suitcase and we rush back to the airport. I make it onto my flight with half an hour to spare. The entire experience is harrowing.

As soon as I'm eligible—about a year after I'm done with grad school—I apply for a green card so I can stay more permanently without the hassle of visas, maybe one day get citizenship, vote, join political parties, participate in protests without being terrified about getting arrested—all things that Americans get to do without worrying about being deported. I know what my staying entails: becoming a part of the settler colonialist project that is this country, contributing toward imperialist wars with my taxes, becoming complicit in the government-backed abuse of other marginalized people. But I want to stay. Because where would I go?

And then it comes in the mail, my green card that, ironically, is tinted blue. More than a decade after arriving in this country—four student visas, three extensions, two work visas later—I hold the card and the pamphlet that says "Welcome to America" in my hands. And I feel nothing—no jubilation, no joy, no lightness, not even a sense of resolution that this saga is behind me. It doesn't magically go away, this feeling of not being from here, that I might be asked to leave at any moment, of being trapped. I suspect it never will.

VIII.

Thankfully, my friends don't stay in their marriages. My cousin lasts the longest: four years, mostly because she's sure she can change her husband, but he doesn't change and one day she's had enough and she leaves. My neighbor friend leaves as soon as her husband hits her child: something protective and angry kicks in and there's no convincing her to stay, she's done. My friend in Seattle gets a divorce and then a new job in Phoenix. She starts afresh, gets back in touch with her old friends, makes a new set of friends she loves—all Muslim divorcées, all women who have stood up for themselves and left.

And Asiyah. I don't know what happens to Asiyah. I scour the Quran and hadith for clues, but there's nothing there, nothing concrete. The pharaoh eventually dies, drowns in the Red Sea that Musa parts with his stick, and the assumption is that Asiyah's story comes to an end here, even if she lives on.

But in my mind, long before Musa parts the Red Sea, Asiyah leaves. She gathers the money she has been putting aside, saddles her favorite horse, and slips away, hidden by the night and the legions of people she's been kind to. Not only does she leave Pharaoh, she leaves Egypt altogether. The pharaoh is too busy fighting Musa to notice, and by the time he does, it's too late, she's gone. To a land far away, somewhere else, anywhere else.

And I. I gather my resentment, my fury that there's nowhere in the world that's magically free of racism and Islamophobia, homophobia and transphobia. I take that burning energy and channel it toward new, different questions: How can I fight injustices in this place where I have community, where I'm choosing to stay? How can I build a life here that feels, rooted in my principles, even if it will never be perfect? Like Muhammad, I ask myself whom do I build with? Like Maryam, I ask myself how do I live?

The Asiyah of my imagination asks herself these questions, too. Builds a life based on her principles—principles that I've heard in my mother's stories about her: kindness for everyone, compassion, and justice. And after she's had time to heal, she meets someone else. Someone who could not be more different from the pharaoh. Someone who is loving and tender and gentle with her bruises, who massages her feet and braids her hair. She lives with this person in a small house with a garden, adopts more babies, leads a happy and fulfilling life in a community that loves her, that fights injustice with her.

When Musa is done fighting the pharaoh, he looks all over the land for his adopted mother. Allah helps him find Asiyah in her small house in a land far away. Musa returns to visit them all the time, bringing his children and their children, and then one day when she's old and ready to go, Asiyah dies peacefully in her sleep. Allah gives her the house in paradise that she asked for, and it's a lot like the house in which she died. The end.

PART
III

NUH

I.

It's Eid morning, around 7 A.M. I should be on a bus, an hour into the journey upstate to my uncle's house, but instead I'm at home, firmly ensconced in my bed.

"Tell me your symptoms again?" my uncle says through the phone, his voice concerned and full of care.

I make myself groan loudly. "My stomach hurts really bad. Like a scrunching kind of pain. And I feel like I'm going to vomit." I throw in a couple of coughs at the end of my sentence.

"That sounds terrible. You're right, it definitely doesn't make sense to travel if you're feeling like this."

I can hear my two- and five-year-old cousins in the background: *Is she coming? Why can't she come? But why not? Ask her why not?* At this time on Eid mornings, I'm usually being woken up by them, jarred into consciousness with their high-pitched yells of *wake up wake up,* their little fingers prying open my eyelids, their nonstop chatter about dresses and presents and the family Eid treasure hunt that my uncle organizes.

"I'm so sorry, Chacha," I croak into the phone. "I really wanted to come."

And I really am sorry, I really did want to go. It'll be the first Eid since I moved to this country five years ago that I won't be spending with him and his family, my closest relatives on this side of the ocean. Even though they had met me all of once before I showed up at the airport needing a ride to college and instructions on how to live in America, they had immediately treated me like a core part of their family—insisting that I spend all holidays with them, sending me home with tubs and tubs of leftovers, calling to check in on me.

"It's okay," my uncle says. "Your health is so much more important. You should rest. We'll really miss you."

And I'll miss them, too; I already do. It's just that—Well. It's just that there's this girl. This girl I call as soon as I hang up on my uncle.

"Did it work?" she says, her voice sleepy with an undercurrent of excitement. She has coached me through my first time lying at the embarrassingly old age of twenty-two. She has talked me through what to say and given me pointers and role-played with me the night before.

"Worked like a charm. Meet you at Eid prayer?"

"Are you sure you're not too sick to leave your bed?"

"Shut up."

I met this girl at the Islamic center at an iftar, all of twenty-eight days ago. I had moved to New York for grad school a few days before Ramadan and found myself four hours away from everyone I knew. I was lonely, and the prospect of breaking my fast alone was depressing, so I made myself go to the Islamic center. On the second day of Ramadan, this girl and I sat next to each other with our plates piled high with food. It was clear that she was lonely, too, that she wasn't in one of the mosque cliques, either. So I friend-chased her. Got her number and texted her the next day, invited her to Taraweeh prayers, to an off-Broadway play, to the suhoor event at IHOP that popped up on my Facebook timeline.

And, surprisingly, she friend-chased me back. Came to all of the things I invited her to, took me to her favorite bubble tea spots in the city, helped me pick up the used furniture I bought on craigslist for my first time furnishing my own room. Suddenly we were breaking our fasts together every evening—at the Islamic center or at a restaurant or getting takeout and picnicking in a park. Suddenly we were praying next to each other at the mosque every day. And suddenly somewhere in the past month, I developed feelings for her, inconvenient feelings that won't go away. Feelings that I'm beginning to understand the contours of, since coming out to Cara two years ago, but feelings that I don't know quite what to do with. What I do know is this: even when we're not hanging out, we end up exchanging so many one-line emails about our days that my in-box runs out of storage. This girl teases me about my dessert obsession. I tease her for going to a bougie gym. The banter is torturously exquisite. These feelings that I have? I have them bad.

But so far, I've kept them to myself. All month, I've quashed them, repeated the arguments to myself over and over. One, there's no indication she's gay, gayish, or even curious. She's never talked about girls like that (*but she's never talked about boys like that, either,* I can't help thinking, before telling myself, over and over, to stop going down this path). Two, I've known her all of twenty-eight days. I don't actually know her that well, don't quite know her politics yet. She could be homophobic for all I know. (*Don't fuck this up,* I tell myself. *She could out you to the Muslims you're trying so hard to befriend. Don't lose the one friend you have in this city.*) Three, it's Ramadan, the month of virtue and restraint, which we've spent fasting, praying, and reading the Quran together. I'm not about to corrupt the chastity of this month with these inconvenient feelings that will probably pass.

But Ramadan is finally over, and if anything, these feelings have only grown stronger and more inconvenient. Which is why on Eid, at the culmination of this month, it feels unfair to have to go away to visit family. After this month of seeing each other almost every day, after this difficult month of prohibition and patience that we have weathered together, how enormously unfair it would be to not celebrate Eid together. In the days leading up to Eid, we talk about how unfair it is. We take steps to rectify the situation, me learning from her intimate, impish tutelage how to play hooky from my family, while she plays hooky from work. So that on the first day of the rest of the year, we end up where it all began: at the Islamic center, for Eid prayer. Together.

She lives closer to the Islamic center than I do so she's there first. I see her before she sees me; she's off to the side, leaning against a tree and scrolling through her phone. She's dressed more fashionably than she has been all month, in a long black skirt that kisses the tops of her ankles—the length just barely appropriate for mosque—and a leopard print blouse. On her head is a silky black hijab set looser than it was all Ramadan. She looks so good I'm embarrassed by my haphazardly ironed button-down, my one pair of nice jeans, my scuffed Converse shoes. But her face lights up when she sees me and I'm unprepared for the rush of affection and shyness I feel. I'm unprepared for the tenderness that fills me when I realize she's waiting outside so we can go into Eid prayer together. I'm so touched it hurts.

We pray next to each other, shoulder to shoulder, foot to foot. Fidget next to each other during the interminable Eid sermon, and then hug and say Eid Mubarak afterward. I'm still shy, but she holds on to me after the hug. Grabs my arm and steers me away from the brunch table at the Islamic center, away from the Dunkin' Donuts and stale jalebi and suffocating hugs from aunties that I've come to associate with the holiday.

"We have the whole day together," she says. "We can't waste stomach space on subpar food. What we're going to do with our day is eat our way around the city!" She leads me outside, into the bright daylight. And I follow.

Our first stop is Sam's falafel in the West Village, just around the corner from the mosque. Growing up in an Arab country has made me a falafel snob, but she insists that the food at this deli is delicious, tells me that the owner is super chatty about his youth boxing career and doles out a generous Muslim discount. And she's right, the falafel is the best I've had in the U.S.—prepared exactly the way I like it, with more fava beans than chickpeas, copious cilantro and parsley dyeing the crumbly insides green.

"You look like you used to be an athlete," I say to the guy behind the counter after he tells us his name is Sami, not Sam. "Maybe something like track or boxing?" His eyes widen in excitement; he gives us free baklava and regales us with stories from his boxing days. She pinches me under the table. I avoid looking at her so I won't burst into giggles.

Our next stop is nowhere in particular. Neither of us has anything specific to do, anywhere to be. What a treat to be out in the city like this, to be outside during the day, able to eat during the day, to be playing hooky on this cool day in the early fall. We meander up Broadway. It's cold and she's underdressed, so I give her my hoodie. She takes my arm and pulls me close for warmth.

We pass by a department store. It's Dhuhr time and clothing store fitting rooms—private and just big enough to kneel in—are the best for discreet praying so I request a pit stop for the second prayer of the day.

"I don't pray regularly—especially when I'm not at home," she says, "But you should go ahead!"

I'm not surprised; she has been dropping hints all month that she's mostly a Ramadan Muslim, but I'm a little disappointed that we won't be squeezing into a small fitting room together.

"That's cool," I say, and grab a few shirts to pretend to try on. When I'm done praying, I find her browsing the racks with a big pile of clothes in her arms that she wants to try on.

"Do you mind? It's Eid and it's sunnah to wear something new!" She grins at me, half-guilty, half-unapologetic. I settle into the patient boyfriend chair near the fitting room for a fashion show—her words, not mine.

It's not until the fashion show begins that I realize I'm a goner. She comes out in cute dress after cute dress, hijab-less now that we're a safe distance away from the Islamic center. Twirling and swishing and posing, she wants opinions on what looks good, what's too short, what's too tight, what has a neckline that's too low. I'm speechless. Partially because I don't know, I don't actually know anything about dresses or how to give clothing advice. But mostly because I'm expending all my energy to keep my face from betraying what I'm feeling. *She's probably straight,* I repeat to myself over and over.

We leave the store overloaded with bags. She proclaims that we need dessert; all that shopping has made her hungry. We get a slice of blueberry pie and eat it on a bench in Madison Square Park, the orange and yellow leaves a respite from the corporate grays of the neighborhood we've passed through. Lean brown squirrels watch us trading bites from the pie until all that's left is a crumb. She halves the crumb and passes it back. I halve the half crumb and pass it back. We pass it back and forth, giggling and taking half bites until she drops the minuscule crumb because she's laughing so hard. She's trying to find it in the grass when my phone rings. It's my uncle.

I pick up, praying that the sounds of the city stay low.

"How are you feeling?" he asks.

"A little better," I say, and this girl moves closer, nestles into me so she can hear what my uncle is saying. I cough a few times into the phone and she taps me on my shoulder, motions not to overdo it. She's coached me that lies are more believable when they're less dramatic.

"Are you outside somewhere?" my uncle says. Shit. I'm on the verge of panic, but she's so good at this, this girl. She motions at me to keep calm and she mimes eating food.

"Yeah, just left the house to get some soup," I say.

"Oh, that's such a good idea. I'm so sorry you're spending Eid like this, all alone."

"Yes," I say, trying to sound sad and not like I'm having the perfect Eid. Magical, even. She gestures at me to wrap up the phone call and I do. She tells me to note this important principle for lying: that shorter conversations mean fewer opportunities to fuck up.

We hang out for a bit in the park, watching the squirrels and pigeons fight over food. By the time we're ready to leave, the day has begun to wane. We're meandering still, talking about everything and nothing, an infinitely looping conversation that feels easy, like we've known each other for twenty-eight lifetimes instead of days. We take a break from walking and sit on the steps of the big post office on Thirty-second Street. She sits close to me. I can feel her thigh through her thin skirt, her arm that is somehow on the step above us but still around me, her hand resting gently on my shoulder. *This is what friends who are girls do,* I tell myself. *She's straight. Stop reading into this.*

She wants to get dinner next, go to the West Side pier to watch the sun set, make our way to Central Park and play spot the raccoon. But I'm full, still unused to eating during the day. I'm happy, reveling in this physical closeness, the way she's always somehow casually touching me. I'm blissfully tired, content to sit on these steps and talk in the fading light of the day.

It's the perfect spot for people watching. We take turns making up stories about the passersby. Mine are all mundane and sad: *here's this man, he's an accountant who had a long day at work, he's going home to watch TV with his boyfriend before he goes to sleep and wakes up and does it all over again.* Her stories waver between being dark and silly: *this woman bought flowers for her husband, they just got news that he's officially in remission from cancer, but she's cheating on him with his boss and is going to leave him tomorrow.*

I'm still laughing at the story about the woman with flowers when she pokes me and points toward a guy who's walking by.

"Hey, I think he's really cute. Do you think he's cute?"

"Not really," I say. I will myself to say more, hint that maybe that he's not my type, that maybe his entire gender is not my type, but the words get stuck in my throat. Stuck behind a ball of reasons and stakes and consequences. What comes out is less direct.

"Are there any guys in your life?" I ask, every cell in my body thrumming in anticipation of her answer.

"Nah."

I gather up all my courage. "Or girls? I didn't mean to be heteronormative."

She stops and looks at me, confused.

"What does heteronormative mean?"

Oh.

Oh. I've been telling myself she's straight all month, but this is the moment I definitively know. Everything goes gray. Time slows as my mind strains to process this information, my body going numb to try to protect myself from feeling this bitter disappointment. The touching doesn't mean anything, the hanging out, the wanting to be around me, the modeling clothes for me doesn't mean anything, can't mean anything if she doesn't even know the word "heteronormative."

She nudges me, asks again what heteronormative means. I stumble through defining it, distracted, trying to remember how to make sounds with my mouth. She laughs at me, tells me that I'm a nerd for using a word with so many syllables. I successfully make a sound that sounds like a laugh. She asks me if I'm hungry yet, is it time for dosas?

But I'm not hungry, I'm a fool. I make some excuse about being tired, about having an early morning tomorrow, so I can go home and try to survive the wave of grief that's waiting for me.

We take the train back to our respective homes. We're going a few stops in the same direction and she maneuvers us into two seats next to each other. Puts her head on my shoulder and closes her eyes, tells me to wake her up when it's her stop. Her body burrows into mine, and a part of my brain screams, *See? See? She can't be straight, she just doesn't know herself. Don't give up yet.* But the rational part of me says different. *She's straight, Lamya,* I tell myself, trying to avoid looking at the blurry reflection of our two bodies in the window across the train. *She's straight. You can't change her.*

II.

Thousands of years ago, God sends a people a prophet: a man by the name of Nuh. They're people who have gods already, gods that their ancestors prayed to for rain and luck and peace. But Nuh comes to them with a religion that's entirely different. One God, no idols, and a moral code. Be kind. Don't cheat each other. Redistribute your wealth to the poor.

Nuh tries to convert the people to Islam. He invites them both publicly and privately, during the day and at night, patiently and then even more patiently, to this religion that he believes in, that feels real and right and rooted in love—of God, of people, of good.

The people hate it. All of it: his message, his God, him. Some make fun of Nuh, of his followers, most of whom are weak and oppressed and the most marginalized in the land. Some of the people don't want to hear what he's saying; they put their fingers in their ears and close their eyes. Others are scared of shaking up their lives. Scared of the upheaval that would come with converting, the stigma, the earth-shattering consequences of being different. They want to live like their parents lived: comfortable lives, familiar lives, lives they see others living, that they know how to live.

For a long time, Nuh persists. Tirelessly continues to call his people, these people that he loves, to God and to good. And somewhere along the line, time elapses and life happens and 950 years go by with nothing to show for his preaching, his patience. *You can't change us,* his people say. *You can't change us.*

III.

You can't change her. She's not gay. This will be my refrain for years, and not just with the girl from the Islamic center, but also with all the other straight girls I find myself in situationships with. *She's not gay, stop waiting for her to come around. You can't make someone less straight by being more perfect. Stop pining. You can't change her.*

And yet. There seems to be no end to the number of straight girls I catch inconvenient feelings for, no end to the amount of effort I put into these situationships, to becoming more perfect in the hopes that somewhere along my string of not-dates with straight girls, one of them will realize that our mutual feelings are not so platonic. That one of them will change.

NOT A DATE #4

There's this girl in the intro to drawing class I'm taking for fun in grad school. Her nose crinkles when she laughs and she skateboards and knows the first two hundred digits of pi. We live near each other and walk back home together after class. Walking becomes talking and talking becomes charged with a confusing tension. We've constantly been promising each other that we'll hang out outside class, and one afternoon we're texting about a TV show we're both watching when we decide that today's the day: we make plans to grab dinner that night. I take her to my favorite South Indian restaurant in the neighborhood. I'm not expecting her to dress up, so I show up in sweats and a raggedy T-shirt. But boy does she dress up. She looks dazzling in a red dress with a deep neckline that I can't stop sneaking glances at. She tells me all about her childhood, asks about mine. Drinks a little and gets touchy-feely, grabs my hand and tells me my long skinny fingers are beautiful, perfect for . . . drawing. She holds up her palm to mine and compares our phalanges. "Doesn't this feel like we're on a date?" she giggles, tipsy and happy. And then goes home, to the boyfriend she lives with.

NOT A DATE #7

There's this girl I know from grad school. Her smile is wide and infectious, and I love hanging out with her because she laughs at all my jokes. Our first semester, we bond over being holiday orphans and having no plans for Christmas. All our friends are out of town and the streets are eerily silent. It feels like we're the only ones left in a postapocalyptic version of this city, so we decide to spend the holidays together.

Christmas day, we find a small diner that has killer veggie burgers. Afterward, we go to her place and watch *The*

Office reruns, sitting thigh to thigh on her couch and cuddling with her new kitten. The entire day is languid. I can't
remember the last time I've spent so many consecutive
hours with someone, and neither of us is in a hurry for it to
end. It gets late and she tells me that I should sleep over,
but there's only one bed in her small studio and I can't tell
what that means because she's always finding ways to mention that she's straight. Even a few minutes ago, as our hands
brushed while petting her kitten, she'd told me that people
are always mistaking her for a lesbian because of how much
she loves cats.

After I leave, I gather all my courage and text her that
she'd make a really good lesbian. That if she ever decides to
play for that team, I want to be first in the draft. She texts
back *lol* and I hold my breath, wondering if she'll say more,
wondering if she'll ask if I'm queer. But she changes the
subject, texts back about the classes we're taking next semester. We never talk about it again.

NOT A DATE #13

House parties are so not my scene, but there's this girl. She's
been trying to persuade me to accompany her to one, a birthday party for her coworker. She's a little wild, this girl: works
a corporate job that hasn't managed to break her total disre-
gard for rules, which I find both terrifying and enthralling. I'm
smitten and would accompany her anywhere, but the per-
suading makes me feel special so I let her wheedle on.

She spends her time at the house party touching my
shoulder, squeezing my arm, pulling me into secret conversations in kitchen nooks. She also spends a lot of time bring-

ing up her straightness, in sentences that otherwise sound suspiciously gay. *Even though I'm straight, I'd totally bang P!nk. I might be straight, but I think men should be rounded up and shot. Unlike most straight women, I'm not afraid to say I love being eaten out.*

We leave the party, arm in arm. Walk around the corner and there is a park, alit in the purple gold of streetlamps against dark sky.

"Let's go in," she says.

"It's locked!" I protest.

She jumps the fence easily. "Don't be so stodgy," she says, and I follow.

She is adamant about not sitting on the grass, so I put my hoodie down as a blanket. She wants to stay a little longer, and a little longer turns into 4 A.M. I'm happy to keep hanging out: the conversation is flowing and I'm curious to see where the night will go. She turns toward me at one point and I think she might kiss me, but she wrestles me instead. We're both athletes so this goes on for a bit until we call a truce. Eventually, she gets hungry. We find a twenty-four-hour deli to get her an egg-and-cheese sandwich that she smothers in hot sauce. After she's done eating, she says she's ready to go home. I'm a little confused, a little disappointed. We take the train in the resplendent light of the early day.

I text her the next day and don't hear back. I text her a socially acceptable three days later and nothing, still nothing. When she finally writes me back two weeks later, it's too late: something has shifted between us. *She's straight. You can't change her,* I've been telling myself, and my refrain has worked and not worked: I've successfully convinced myself to stop pining over her. I've already started flirting with someone else, someone who is probably straight.

"What is it with you and these straight girls?" my Queer Life Mentor, Zu, asks me one day while I'm in the middle of regaling them with stories about my not-dates. We're watching an early round playoff soccer game that's streaming illegally on the laptop in front of us.

"I don't know," I say. "They're just drawn to me, I guess."

"Are they drawn to you or are you drawn to them?" they ask gently, mercifully sparing me eye contact by keeping their gaze on the game.

The directness of the question causes my body to flush with uncomfortable recognition. I shrug and keep my eyes trained on the game, but all I can see now are the faces of my unrequited crushes on unattainable women over the years. My economics teacher in high school. My friend's mom, who was helping me with my applications to grad school. A Zionist, whom I was collaborating with on a project at work, who wanted to argue about Palestine whenever we were done looking at data. One of the cocaptains of my soccer team in college, who was dating the cocaptain of the men's soccer team. My occupational therapist, as she walked me through exercises for my broken finger. They were all straight women, all femmes, all into banter and flattered by the attention I gave them. I flirted with them and they flirted back, partly—if not entirely—because I wasn't a guy, because nothing would happen, because they weren't interested in me like *that*. So they would platonically cuddle with me, call me crying about their trash boyfriends, sleep curled up next to me in my bed, text me when they were drunk to tell me I'm better than a boyfriend, and if only I were a guy they would date me.

I've told Zu a lot of these stories and it's annoying that they remember them so well.

"Lamya, a lot of people go through phases with straight girls," they say. "But if we're counting high school you're on, what, your second decade? It might be worth thinking through where this is coming from."

I had courted Zu as my Queer Life Mentor precisely because they're so perceptive and astute and don't hold back saying exactly what they think. Now, though, these qualities are annoying. I choose not to respond, hoping the game will distract them and the conversation will end there.

But Zu takes their mentoring duties very seriously, and as the game winds down, they push me to think through the underlying issues, asking what stops me from crushing on, asking out, going on dates with queer women who would be interested in dating me. Like the soccer players on the screen, I answer mostly in grunts and vague head movements.

"You know I struggled with internalized homophobia for a long time," Zu says. "It's hard not to absorb the fucked-up shit we grew up hearing about queerness. Could it be that?"

"That must be it," I say, ready for this conversation to be over, ready to go back to the six kinds of chips on the table and the last few minutes of this game. Besides, they're right; of course I'm scared that dating queer women will make my gayness real in ways it isn't when I'm crushing on straight girls. And there are so many people to hide from: my Muslim community in New York, my grandma, who has now moved in with my uncle four hours away, my parents across the ocean. Rejection from straight girls is so much easier than rejection from my entire family and religion. It doesn't help that I am totally, absolutely, definitely intimidated by all the badass queer femmes I know.

But then, a few months later, a woman who I know for a fact is gay tells me she likes me, and suddenly I'm not so sure that my hesitance is the result of internalized homophobia alone. She's a sweetheart, this woman: we meet at a queer Muslim retreat, where we attend workshops together and hang out talking a few times on the porch. I find her adorable. Surprisingly, she finds me adorable, too. I discover this because on day three of the retreat, she tells her friend, who tells my friend, who tells me, and just like that, I stop finding her adorable. Now that she knows that I know she thinks I'm adorable, I have to deal with it—and I deal with it by being angry. That what could have been a fun, flirty friendship is now over. And on top of that, we're stuck at a retreat together with a dozen mutual friends who know about our mutual finding each other adorable. I'm angry that I now have to contend with the messiness and fallout of what we are or aren't going to do with our feelings. I'm angry that I have to continue to be in community with her. My anger comes on so quickly and strongly that it surprises me. I feel nauseous and spend the last day of the retreat hiding in my room, sick with a "stomach bug."

I do a lot of thinking while I'm hiding, and eventually realize why I like crushing on straight girls. They're easy, they're predictable. Their rejection is preordained: so familiar that it makes the uncomfortable comfortable, normal, expected—even safe. With straight girls, I get to choose being rejected, I get to reject myself. But having feelings for another queer person makes the situation feel entirely out of my control; I wouldn't know if or when or why they'd reject me, and what's scarier is that I don't know what I'd do if they *didn't* reject me. I'm too afraid to find out.

IV.

My friend Manal is feisty. We've been in constant touch since praying next to each other at the LGBTQ+ mixer three years ago, and not a week goes by without us getting dinner or going to a lecture or event together. Today we're at an Ethiopian restaurant after an underwhelming talk on Muslim feminism at our Islamic center, where the speaker had the nerve to say that not all feminists are lesbians, that we should take into account not scaring off Muslim men. Manal is not a laid-back person—it's one of my favorite things about her—and a combination of the unimpressiveness of the lecture and our irate, pointed questions to the speaker has made her extra feisty. At dinner, while I'm ruing a failed nondate with a straight girl I once took to the restaurant we're at, she turns that feistiness in my direction.

"You have got to stop going on all these nondates," she announces.

"What?" I ask, thoroughly surprised. She had laughed at all the appropriate parts in my straight-girl story, and I thought she had been enjoying it.

"Khalas, Lamya, I've heard what, twenty or thirty of these stories and zero actual date stories. This has got to be taking a toll on you. You have got to start going on real dates."

"I will, I will, I swear." I say this automatically every time anyone—Billy, Manal, my Queer Life Mentor—bugs me about dating.

"What apps are you on?" Manal asks. "Give me your phone. I want to see your profiles."

"Um, I'm not on any . . ." I say, startled by how quickly this conversation has turned real.

"Okay, that's totally unacceptable. We're going to download some right now." She sits back in her chair and holds out her hand for my phone.

"I'll do it when I get home, promise," I say, trying to laugh in a way that sounds casual and not terrified. "What should we order? Should we split a veggie combo?"

"Stop deflecting. You're going to do it right now. I'm not going to order until you at least download Tinder."

"But I'm hungry!" I protest. "It's getting late! I had an early lunch!"

"Too bad."

"Okay, let's order and then I swear I'll download it while our food is being prepared."

"Nope," Manal says, crossing her arms and sending away the server when he approaches. Of course, my stomach chooses that moment to growl audibly.

"Fine, fine, *fine*," I say, trying to sound more playful than annoyed, trying to disguise the combination of terror and thrill I feel about actually, really doing this. Because yes, Manal is stubborn and I want to order, but also because somewhere along the way, time has elapsed and life has happened and I'm almost thirty years old and I've never been in a relationship.

That is how I find myself on my first date. Or, more accurately, how I find myself waiting forty minutes for my date to show up. *Is this what all dates are like?* I text Zu at the thirty-minute mark. *Sometimes!* they write back. *You should know by now that queers are always late! Whatever you do, do not leave.* It's like Zu can read my mind: I've been trying to convince myself not to leave for at least thirty-five of the forty minutes I've been waiting. Lateness is one of my pet peeves; all the queer friends I've made in the past couple of years say it has something to do with being a Capricorn. I usually have a thirty-minute rule, after which I leave. I've been trying to use this as an exercise in boundaries—the first time I waited an hour for a friend, I was irritable the entire time we hung out. But this is a first date, and after texting my Queer Life Mentor, I silently add an extra fifteen minutes to my thirty-minute wait limit to signal to the world that I'm trying, I'm really trying to be open to new people and new experiences. To actual dates.

It hasn't been easy, this whole dating apps thing. I match with women I think are cute, but texts back and forth fizzle out without us ever meeting. I get bailed on, I get bored, I swipe to the end of Tinder. This date that I've been waiting forty minutes for is the most promising prospect in a while: gorgeous and smart and angry at the world. We've been messaging back and forth for a few weeks. Small talk at first (*What do you do? How long have you been in the city?*) and then slightly deeper questions (*What's your favorite emoji and why? If you could live anywhere in the world, where would you go?*) We've finally progressed to talking about meeting up and it's taken awhile to fix a date because of our busy work schedules, but here I finally am, in a leather jacket I borrowed from Zu, in front of a Mexican restaurant in the East Village, waiting for my first actual date.

She's incredibly apologetic when she finally arrives. *So sorry, the A train's been acting up, you know,* and I don't know how you can be forty minutes late on rush-hour-frequency trains, but the persistence and sincerity of her apologies make me soften. It doesn't hurt that she has a sexy voice, deep and tinged with a soft Nigerian lilt. And it definitely does not hurt that she's even more beautiful than she was in her pictures: tall and lithe, small fro, an open smile. She's wearing a leather jacket, too, but hers fits her in all the ways that leather jackets are supposed to fit, snug and worn in. "Great jacket," I tell her. She looks at mine, almost exactly the same as hers, and laughs.

We walk into the restaurant. Or try to. She insists that I go in first, but I'm already holding the door and don't understand why she can't just walk in. We tussle like that for a few seconds, stopping and starting. Eventually I defuse the awkward tension with a laugh and walk inside. But this happens again when we try to order at the counter. "You go first," she says. I'm not ready, but she insists that she'll wait.

I stand my ground and win this round of whatever competitive game this is that I'm not sure why we're playing. She orders and then I sneak in and try to pay for both of us because that's what my Queer Life Mentor has taught me to do on dates. But she is stubborn about paying, too. We go back and forth for a bit, neither of us budging, and then finally decide to split the check.

We find a table. She has to go to the bathroom, and while she's gone, I take a second to breathe and try to reset. I don't understand how most of the evening so far has become a battle to out-nice each other. I get up, stretch my legs, get us sauces and condiments from the counter, and sit back down. I see her leave the bathroom and then she disappears. I'm trying to figure out if she can't remember where we're sitting and if I should rescue her when she comes by a few minutes later bearing the same sauces and condiments I've already gotten us. We both laugh—a little more hesitatingly this time. We end up with a lot of sauces on our table, but it's great because it turns out we both like our food extra spicy. She takes off her jacket as she settles in, and that's when I realize we're both wearing the same outfit: leather jackets, dark jeans, gray button-downs, and dyke boots, hers black and mine blue. She's wearing a black beanie and I'm wearing a black hijab, but *fuck*. I can't tell if she doesn't notice or if she doesn't let on. I, on the other hand, can't stop glancing at her to confirm that this is really happening. I put all my energy into not freaking out.

We're different people, don't get me wrong—this becomes obvious when we start talking. She watches TV, a lot of it, whereas I don't have the attention span to watch more than twenty minutes at a time or the stomach to sit through the kind of violence that is commonplace in all of the shows she names. She grew up as the only Black person and only immigrant in a rural town in the Midwest, and I grew up in a large multiracial city in a rich Arab country. She loves going out, loves dancing and gay bars and letting loose on weekends. I hate places where it's too loud to have conversations and don't dance because I have the coordination and grace of a wooden stick. She pauses between words and sentences for emphasis, and I drown in the silences.

And then there's this. She tells me that she's just gotten out of a long relationship—six years of ups and downs, a breakup that had been a long time coming. But it's not the breakup that bothers me—it's that in all her stories so far, there has been a "we." I hadn't noticed this before, but now it dawns on me that this invisible person in our conversation so far—about TV shows and things to do in the city and rural America—has been her ex.

All at once, this whole evening seems like an astronomically bad idea. All of it—this meal, this date—hasn't been going well, and I don't know why I've been forcing it and I don't want to be here anymore. We're way too different, and yet somehow way too similar, too used to interacting with dates in the same ways, too clashing in the similarities of our butch energies. Claustrophobia wells up within me and I feel an urgent need to leave. I finish eating quickly, don't even get a to-go box for my leftover fries. Tell her I'm really sorry but my friend just texted and needs help with something, it's a friend-emergency, I'm so sorry, I have to go. "No problem," she says. "It was so nice to meet you, I'd love to see you again." She puts on her leather jacket, then we get up and walk out of the restaurant, bumping into each other as we open the door to leave, as we each try to convince the other to go first. Outside, she puts her hand on my back to guide me and I jump. "I'll text you," I say. And I know, I *know*, I should have texted her the next day, something about how nice it was to meet her and let's just be friends, something like that. But I don't. I'm just done.

V.

After 950 years of trying to change people, Nuh, too, is done. Breaks down one day and admits this to God, confesses that he is tired of trying to convert people who are uninterested, of being mocked, of being unsuccessful. God listens. And in response, God tells Nuh to build an ark. Not just any ark, a big ark, a giant ship in a city in the middle of the desert. God tells Nuh to build this structure for which there is no use in this place with no body of water for thousands of miles. Did Nuh wonder if it was a test from God? Like I wonder about the people I've been texting, the dates I'm going on? This building of an ark, this exercise in futility?

Whatever his reservations, Nuh accepts God's command. Builds an ark a little every day, plank by plank, nail by nail. His people call him a madman, make fun of the pointlessness of his task. Which it is: an exercise in futility, yes, but also of hope. This slow building of an escape—from preaching, from waiting, from the circles Nuh's life has been stuck in. It's an act of boundless optimism, of absolute trust in God. So certain is Nuh of better times to come that he puts all his time and energy and resources into this enormous endeavor. This giant ship in the middle of the desert, no seas for thousands of miles.

VI.

Like Nuh, I keep trying. I continue to go on dates and engage in this exercise of futility.

BAD DATE #3

Manal drags me to a speed dating event. *For moral support,* she says, but I know she's taking me because she thinks I need multiple avenues to put myself out there. "Out there" is an after-hours bookstore full of women who like women who like books. It couldn't be more intimidating.

My first three-minute date is unmemorable, but the second woman is kind of cute. She's a librarian with striking blue eyes that contrast with her dark hair and pale skin. I tell her how I used to organize my books alphabetically but now I arrange them by color. Her eyes widen and she leans across the table toward me. "Oh wow," she says. "Tell me more!"

"Well, it's not as easy as you'd think because color doesn't fall on a linear spectrum. And there are too many white books in the world."

"You should intersperse the white books throughout your bookshelf. You know, like a white book every other book?"

"I don't know if I'd be able to do that because, well, metaphor."

Her face turns even whiter, which should be my sign to stop but I don't.

"I've thought about putting all the white books on a separate shelf or something."

She laughs awkwardly, shuffles in her seat.

"Or in a box under my bed."

"Are you telling me that you're not into white . . . books?"

Fortuitously, the buzzer rings signaling the end of the date and I'm spared the rest of this conversation. Later, as we're both leaving, we pass each other and studiously avoid eye contact. Later still, a few months afterward, we run into each other at a friend's lesbian movie night and pretend to have never met.

BAD DATE #5

She picks a coffee shop uptown, halfway between hers and mine. It's a cute spot: a tiny, new café still in the process of figuring itself out. It's minimalist, with very little seating for the zero customers who are there that Friday evening we meet up, with mood lighting and dim décor that clashes with the cheesy pop music playing in the background. Behind the counter is one bored barista close enough to shamelessly eavesdrop on our conversation. I'm in love with this coffee shop.

She's cute, too, my date. Soft eyes and a playful grin. A striking red streak in her dark hair that must have been recently acquired because she keeps playing with it. Gestures languid and graceful, one adorably positioned asymmetrical tooth. We met online, but once we start talking, realize that we've seen each other at various Asian American organizing events, that we have friends in common. The conversation flows easily, about writing and art and being from Not Here. Life and displacement stories and the ways in which we carve space in our communities. An hour passes and I don't even notice.

But we're not attracted to each other. That ends up being clear in the way we part: awkwardly, abruptly, a half-way hug and no promise to meet up soon. We exchange email addresses, but we're both cognizant, and cognizant of each other's cognizance, that we're not going to be reaching out to each other. It's been a pleasant evening, fun even, but there's just no chemistry.

It's not that she's not my type—she is, she's femme and political and a little bit weird. It's not that we don't have things in common—we do. It feels entirely nonsensical that I'm not interested in her. What is wrong with me? I start to wonder if I'm straight. Sometimes people go half a lifetime and realize they're gay; there's no reason I couldn't have been straight all along. I have an existential crisis for a day or two, panic, and then call Billy, who reminds me that to be straight I'd have to like men. Crisis averted, I resume swiping through my queer dating apps.

BAD DATE #6

An ice cream date, in the early evening. The second thing she asks me is, how are you queer and Muslim at the same time? I take a second to roll my eyes in my head and then give her what seems to me an entirely reasonable, level-headed, paragraph-long answer. Afterward she says, "Damn, I need a PowerBar after talking to you."

BAD DATE #7

A poetry reading, Claudia Rankine in fact, a litmus test kind of date. She tells me afterward at dinner that the poetry made her uncomfortable, that not all white people are privileged, that the reading portrayed white people as evil. I leave without even getting dessert.

BAD DATE #9

A lunch date, Thai food in the West Village. She tells me she's moving in three weeks. To Uganda, for at least a year but possibly indefinitely. There is no second date.

BAD DATE #12

Dean Spade is giving a lecture and I have an extra ticket so I invite her. She bails on me the day before, says she double-booked. Almost two years of online dating has taught me when to cut my losses. There is no first date.

VII.

God knows that sometimes you need to destroy the cycles you're caught in, that sometimes you need to wipe the slate clean and start over. So God sends Nuh a flood. Opens the gates to the heavens and lets it rain, and dear God, does it rain. The streams swell. The valleys flood. Water pours from the sky and doesn't let up until the world is covered, the mountains sink, and there's water as far as the eye can see. God sends a flood, and the ark saves Nuh and his followers and the animals, two by two, in pairs. After all of the waiting, the 950 years of preaching, God sends Nuh a reset. This ark in the middle of the desert, which was mocked as an act of futility, becomes a reprieve, a chance to start over.

I, too, am in need of a flood. Twoish decades of pining after straight girls and I'm done. Two years of going on dates with queer women, two years of bad dates that leave me sad and angry and tired and undeniably over it. I'm done with dating forever, I decide. "Isn't that a bit dramatic?" asks Zu. "Are you sure that's a good idea?" Billy questions. "You know, you could always take a break just for a year or two," says Manal. But I'm sure. I don't need a partner: I have my friends, my queer Muslim community, my cat. I have my work, my writing, and a reliable vibrator. I don't need a partner. I've tried everything, and I'm done. I need to escape from the cycles I'm caught in. I need to start over. And then I go on one last date.

VIII.

GOOD DATE #1

Her name is Olivia, but she goes by Liv. We've been trying to meet up for a while. It takes forever to set a date, and when the day comes, there's a storm—a freezing rain turned to hail, grocery-store-shelves-emptied and everyone-huddled-indoors kind of storm.

How do you feel about ice cream in the winter? I text her.

Liv doesn't know that this is a test, but she passes. Says she's definitely into ice cream in the winter and agrees to meet in the storm, even chooses the option that involves traveling a little farther for better ice cream. She shows up on time, despite inclement weather trains, and I'm already swooning. We talk about her dissertation, her love for this city, how she left and then moved back. She asks me questions about myself, a strong indication that this might not be a bad date. I talk about this book of short stories I'm reading by a Pakistani writer. "Oh, is it Manto?" she asks, this white girl from Vermont, and my swooning intensifies. I'm having such a good time that I forget to check my watch and end up hanging out way later than I had planned.

GOOD DATE #2

I take Liv out to dinner, and afterward, to a friend's play. At the Szechuan restaurant I take her to, we share a hot pot at the spiciest level possible and I'm impressed that her tolerance matches mine, despite her self-professed daily diet of salads and chopped cheese. "Yum!" she says, reaching for more food, as both of our noses run and tongues go numb. I'm thoroughly enjoying myself. On our walk to the theater, we talk about how national parks are a product of American expansionism and white supremacy—and guiltily admit to each other that we still want to visit every single one. I am so charmed. We get dessert afterward. My apartment is just around the corner, but I wait with her at the stop until her bus comes, not wanting the conversation to end, not wanting the evening to end.

GOOD DATE #4

We go to a lecture on queer history at the New York Public Library. All my friends think it's a terrible idea: Who takes a date to a nerd lecture? But my instincts are spot-on. Liv is a nerd, too. I'm about to apologize in advance for taking notes during the lecture, but then I see her guiltily whip out a journal for the same reason. We end up in Grand Central Station afterward for dessert. She leads me to a nook that is both private and public and we sit on the floor, talking till late and inching closer to each other.

GOOD DATE #7

Liv cooks me dinner, a three-course meal that she's nowhere near done with when I show up. I bring her flowers, help her chop herbs and finish cooking. She bakes me brownies. Later on, I gather up the courage to kiss her for the first time.

IX.

Eventually, the rains stop and the sun comes out, and Nuh's ark settles back down on land. Nuh and his followers alight into a changed world, ready to build anew—differently this time: a community that is based on their principles, a community rooted in hope.

And I—I don't know yet if I've landed in a new world. But I do know that like Nuh, God sends me a flood—and with my cynicism and hopelessness washed away, I can let in this feeling of hope. Like at fourteen, when my curiosity about Maryam turned my eyes to a horizon I didn't think I was interested in, I'm ready to meet my new world. I'm ready to keep seeing Liv, keep seeing where our dates go. Maybe even build something anew.

YUSUF

I.

I am thirty-two years old when I reread Surah Yusuf. I've read it before, of course: I've been *reading* reading the Quran for decades now. Not just the Arabic of my childhood readings, not cursory translations, not processed tafsirs chock-full of unacknowledged conjecture, but readings that are my own. Slow readings that meander, one verse at a time with deep reflection. Sometimes quick sprint reads, all thirty juz' in thirty days in Ramadan, for the bonus blessing of finishing the whole book in the month. Sometimes they're Quran study readings with my queer Muslim crew, our comfort ayahs or a few verses chosen from the book cracked open at random, passages that we journal about and then share thoughts on as a group. Other times, they're readings where I imagine God speaking directly to me, the verses a conduit for our connection. Messy readings that allow me to be both enraged and inspired at the same time by this living text, this breathing text—as the living, breathing me.

Every reading feels different, but this rereading of Surah Yusuf feels especially so. I'm reading with Manal, who has become one of my best friends in the six years since our fortuitous meeting at the LGBTQ+ mixer. We've been slowly making our way through the Quran, the result of a random conversation at a friend's birthday dinner party. The dinner was a big step in my relationship with Liv—it was the first time she was meeting a lot of my queer Muslim friends—and I had accidentally abandoned her as Manal and I began nerding out about a new tafsir of the Quran. We had both heard a lot of excitement about this tafsir. It was heralded as detailed and progressive and well researched, a compendium of all the tafsirs to date including both Sunni and Shia sources. I had just bought this tafsir in hardcover, and a quick flip through made it seem promising. "We should read it together," I had suggested to Manal casually, not expecting that she would buy it online on her phone right then and there at the dinner table, not expecting that we would peel away from the other conversations at this dinner to talk about how to decide on our first reading goal, our first meeting time, and our ground rules for reading together.

At the end of the night, as everyone was leaving the potluck, I had to hunt down Liv and finally found her hanging out with a few of my friends on the balcony. "I'm so sorry! I promise I'll make it up to you," I had said. "Oh, and in other news, Manal and I just mapped out how to finish reading the whole Quran in four years."

Two years later, Manal and I are nowhere near halfway through the Quran—more like a third or so into it. But surprising ourselves, we've mostly stuck to our reading goals. Each week, we read ten pages of the tafsir—Arabic and English, text and interpretation—and then every Wednesday morning, we call each other to discuss the ayahs. And in these two years, life has happened: she's moved across the ocean and then back and then once more, halfway across the country. I've moved apartments three times in New York, which feels comparable. We've both finished grad school, we've acquired and lost jobs and pets and tattoos. I've kept dating Liv, and Manal has called it off with her long-term partner—both accomplishments of different kinds. And throughout these years, there's been this thread of constancy: Manal and I read a set of ayahs, and then we call each other to talk.

At first our calls are all business, strictly our time to talk about the Quran. But as the weeks turn into months, our conversations expand. Something begins to shift in our friendship; we share more about our lives than we ever have before. Between discussing verses, she talks to me about difficult things: her parents aging, friend breakups, sex. It's hard for me to share the difficult things in my life, but I try, too: I turn my travails into funny stories so I can slip in the tragic amid the comic. I tell her about fucked-up things that happen at work that I cope with by pretending they're not happening to me but to someone else. Joys are even harder to share, but we start telling each other about those, too: I am ecstatic when she tells me about an award that her dissertation wins, she cheers loudly when my green card finally comes in the mail. We were always friends, but through reading the Quran together, we become family.

It's been useful to feel so close to Manal, because the eleven surahs we've read so far are some of the most difficult in the Quran: full of legal rulings and repetition, dull details and tedium, and two of the surahs are entirely about war. These eleven surahs contain some of the hardest verses to reconcile: the infamous 4:34 verse in Surat al-Nisaa that is interpreted to condone intimate partner violence; the inheritance ayahs that dictate that women get half shares of wealth compared to men; the story of the people of Lut, who were supposedly punished for practicing homosexuality. We find ourselves repeatedly expressing disappointment in the tafsir, which has parroted a lot of patriarchal interpretations of the difficult ayahs without giving credence to women's scholarship, to anti-oppressive interpretations from different schools of thought. We've felt angry, we've felt resigned, we've broken down and close-read verses until they've blurred into each other. We've even come up with our own alternate explanations: What if Allah wants us to abolish inheritance altogether? What if Allah made inheritance deliberately unfair to women because They want women to lead a revolution against the vertical transfer of assets? What if Allah wants us to extrapolate gender inequality to class inequality, wants us to redistribute wealth?

Eleven surahs later, we're finally at Surah Yusuf and it feels like a momentous achievement to have made it this far. We've been counting down the pages to this surah for a while now—only nine weeks to go, only seventy pages to go, until we're one surah away from this melodious surah on the

dramatic story of Yusuf, with its internal rhymes and allit-
eration, poignant moments, twists and turns. We're excited
because this surah marks a turning point in the Quran. The
next section is almost entirely allegorical stories, of brave
and steadfast prophets, of talking animals, of saints come
back from the dead. Stories of persistence, stories of miracles, stories of rewards for those who are patient. The gen-
tler, easier, more inspiring parts of the Quran.

Except, in our eager anticipation, we've forgotten that
there's nothing gentle or easy about the story of Yusuf—a
fact that becomes instantly clear when I sit down to read
the tafsir of the surah.

As a young boy, Yusuf has a dream. He sees stars and the
sun and moon bowing to him. He tells his father, the prophet
Yaakub, who recognizes the dream as a sign that Yusuf is a
prophet. Yaakub begins to dote on Yusuf, whose ten older
brothers become jealous of the attention, of how obvious it
is that Yusuf is the favorite child. So the brothers plot. "Why
don't you trust us with Yusuf?" they ask their father. "Let us
take him out to the desert to play." Their father knows something is awry; he's reluctant to be separated from Yusuf for
even an afternoon, but eventually lets him go. The brothers
take Yusuf to the middle of the desert, away from everyone,
away from everything. And then they beat him up. This
child, this defenseless child, smallest of them all, is beaten
until he's almost dead. They take turns hitting him, almost
break his limbs. Then they tear off his shirt, throw him into
a well, and leave.

Yusuf calls after his brothers, pleads and begs, but they
are unmoved. And so, as he hears their departing footsteps
in the dust, Yusuf resigns himself to his fate: this is where
he is going to die, all alone in this dark, damp well. Meanwhile, the brothers stain Yusuf's shirt with blood from a goat
and bring it back to their father, whom they tell that Yusuf
was mauled by a wolf. "We left him to guard our things and
a wolf got him," they say. "Yusuf is gone now, Yusuf is dead."
Unsaid: *love us instead.*

"So much for gentle, easy, and inspiring, huh?" Manal says
early Wednesday morning when she calls to talk about the
first fifteen verses of Surah Yusuf. I've been working long
hours this week, coming home only to sleep. I've stayed up
after Fajr prayer this morning to review the verses, the details of which are fresh in my mind. This new tafsir pulls
from different sources and describes what Yusuf's brothers
did to him in shocking specificities that I have never before
come across in my decades of reading this surah—perhaps
because they're so violent. I've barely been able to read
through all the descriptions, which are so intense they make
me shudder. By the time Manal calls, my anger at what the
brothers did to Yusuf has calcified.

"Yeah, that was really fucked up," I say, my voice rising
in fury. "I can't believe they took him out to the middle of
the desert and then beat him up and left. Talk about giving
a kid abandonment issues."

"Yeah, definitely. His own brothers did that to him.
Imagine how that would fuck you up."

My voice climbs higher as I get more worked up. "No wonder Yusuf has it so hard the rest of his life. How do you live after that happens to you? How do you ever love anyone again? How do you trust anyone again? That's what I think Yusuf's story is about. Living with the consequences of trauma, of being abandoned."

"You know what's weird, though?" Manal says. "The introduction in the tafsir says that Surah Yusuf is about love. I find that so fascinating. What if we're thinking about it from the wrong angle? What if this surah is about healing instead? What if this surah is about healing from being left? What if it's about healing through love?"

II.

My first coherent memory is of my father leaving. I am young—maybe three or four years old—and it's the middle of the night and I'm sleeping in my favorite nightshirt. It is bright blue and pink and purple and so ugly that my mother only lets me wear it to sleep. My father comes into the bedroom, where the four of us sleep: me and my brother on cots, him and my mother on the big bed. My father wakes me up to say goodbye. I'm groggy and confused: all the lights are on and there are too many noises for the middle of the night, too many footsteps coming and going, too many voices hurried and harried. My father is gentle. Says he's leaving but that we'll join him soon, and I don't understand what's happening or where he's going, but he kisses me and his mustache tickles my cheek. He wakes my brother to say goodbye and then someone is yelling at my father that he's going to be late for his flight and a car outside is honking and then my father is gone. I start crying, but no one notices because my brother is crying louder and, unexpectedly, my mother is crying, too, and my grandmother is at our house, holding her and telling her it'll be okay. And then my nose starts bleeding. I taste the blood on my lips before I see it on my hands and then I start screaming. Someone takes me to the bathroom and holds me over the sink and pinches my nose but it's too late. My favorite nightshirt is ruined.

My second coherent memory is of the rest of us leaving: me and my brother and my mom. Six months after my father leaves, we leave everything and everyone we know to join him, traveling from the country where I was born to the country where I'll live for the next thirteen years of my life. I don't remember the goodbyes or the airplane. But I do remember the arrival, me and my brother playing with the tape barriers in the customs area of the airport, somehow depressingly lit even in this country of blazing sun. I remember knocking my tooth on the carousel while we waited for our luggage, I remember it hurting, and I remember not crying because my mother told me to be brave. I remember the way the heat hit us as we exited the terminal: dry and burning and scorching our skins, unlike the heavier humidity we had known in our old city on the ocean. I remember my father waiting for us at the exit, mustacheless and smiling harder than I had ever seen, leading us to our new car—an old blue Buick he had polished until it shone. I remember him driving us to our new apartment, and the colors of the world outside the car: the grays and browns of the desert, the bright greens of fake trees.

Our new home is not big, but it's bigger than our old place, with two bedrooms instead of one, which means that my brother and I get our own room. It's set up already, with two twin beds that we jump on as soon as my mother leaves us alone. She isn't even mad when she comes back and catches us, just tells us to stop and we do. We go back to exploring the rest of the apartment, which has four air conditioners—three more than we used to have. My father insists that we count them together, tells my brother and me to turn them all on at the same time, that we don't have to ration AC time anymore. The ACs hum to life, fill the apartment with cold air and a background thrum. "Welcome to our new life," I remember my father saying over and over. "Welcome to our new life."

Except our new life is not as exciting as that first day seemed to promise, that first day when my father takes us to a park and then to the grocery store, where my brother and I both get to pick out one toy and a full-sized candy bar each. The newness of our move quickly wears off, replaced by an uncomfortable awareness that everything here is different. For the first time in our lives, we're all alone, the four of us: my brother and I, my mom and my dad. We don't know anyone in this new country besides the men who are my father's bachelor friends: men like him who have come here to work and save up enough money to bring their families over. We don't have any friends, don't speak the language, and can't leave the apartment while my father is at work because my mother can't drive. I miss my old life desperately. I miss my grandmother who lived next door to us and told me I was her favorite. I miss my aunts and uncles who lived a few doors down, my cousins who were everywhere, everyone who was everywhere, all doors open day and night, food and kids going back and forth between the houses. I miss my kindergarten, I miss my friends. I miss evenings at my great-grandmother's house, all her children and their children and their children's children gathered around her as she held court on the bed, the adults talking and flipping through magazines, the kids playing with each other and running around. I miss the park we used to go to with the yellow swings. I miss weekend trips to the beach, everyone squeezed into two cars, sitting on laps. I miss playing in the sand and eating chanachur, everyone yelling at my cousin who would always wade in too far. I miss camel rides and sunsets and the salty wind. I miss being surrounded by love.

I don't deal with it very well, that loss of love. I don't understand it, and no one will explain it to me. Why can't we all go back? Why can't my dad find a job back home? Why can't my grandparents come visit us? Why can't we talk to them on the phone longer? Why is it so expensive to call them? Why can't my mother drive here? Why can't we go outside in the heat? Why are we stuck inside all day? Why won't the Arab kids next door play with us? Why is it so hard to make new friends?

And I have other questions, too, that I can't quite formulate but feel deeply. Why is my brother my mom's favorite? Is it because he's light-skinned and pretty, with long lashes and a quick smile? Is it because he's easygoing and isn't always asking questions? Is it because he's frequently sick, frequently the subject of my mother's worry? It becomes clear in those early days that they're a team, those two, until the evening, when my father comes home and he and my mom become a team and then my brother and I get to be a team. When I was surrounded by family and love, I never even noticed who loved whom more. I had others to love me, others to play with. But now I'm on the outside and I feel it keenly. I feel it every time my mother shows affection to my brother and not me; every time she's easy on him and not me; every time she yells at me and not him for something we both did together; every time she yells at me that I should have known better because I'm the older sister, that I should be taking care of him. One afternoon, I walk into the living room to find her hugging him, a close, sweet hug that I don't recognize. I didn't know that she hugged like that. In my hurt and confusion, I act out, refusing to share toys with my brother, not doing my chores, talking back—which means spanking and punishments, my mother refusing to speak to me for days at a time, no TV.

Things get better once school starts, but only sort of. I make friends easily, but we can't have playdates after school because no one has transportation options while their fathers are at work, and none of that matters anyway because my friends always leave. Every year, without fail, a third of the kids in my class go back to their home countries. We're in the kind of place where people come from all over the world to make money that's not taxed, and once they've saved up enough to build a house or start a business, they leave, go back to their home countries to lead better lives. But as a kid, I don't know all that. All I know is that after first grade, my best friend leaves. After second grade, I leave to go to a new school and have to start over. And then, at the end of every year after that—after third grade, fourth grade, fifth grade—the kid who has become my best friend leaves. In the middle of seventh grade, I leave: my father gets a new job and we move to a city on the other side of the country. It takes me awhile to make friends at this new school. I am tired of starting afresh. When I do finally make a new best friend, she, too, leaves. That is the year that I've had enough of best friends. I make friends, but I make lots and lots of them so I never have to worry about being crushed by any one of them leaving. I crack jokes and pull pranks to draw people toward me, to entertain friends without ever having to share anything intimate. I keep everyone at a bit of a distance, so it's not as crushing when they do inevitably leave. And I stop using the word "best" to describe any of my friends.

III.

The weekend before my next Quran date with Manal, I open the tafsir, less enthusiastically this time, to read what happens after Yusuf's brothers leave him all alone at the bottom of a well in the middle of the desert, bleeding and bruised and barely alive, where he's resigned himself to dying in the damp and the cold.

But long after his brothers have left—hours, days, who knows?—Yusuf hears a sudden noise overhead. Voices clamor above him and then a bucket is lowered into the well. Yusuf grabs on to the bucket, holding it with every last bit of strength he has. When he's near the top, he sees that he is being pulled up and out of the well by people from a passing caravan who saw the well and stopped for water. Imagine their surprise when they draw up a boy.

The people of the caravan are ecstatic—they can sell him as a slave! They take Yusuf with them to a new country—Egypt, far from Yusuf's home, away from his brothers, away from everything he knows. In Egypt, the people of the caravan sell Yusuf to a rich man, a minister to the king. The minister and his wife are childless; they want to raise Yusuf as a son. Finally, some stability in Yusuf's life, a few years of calm.

Yusuf grows up in the minister's house. He is obedient and respectful, and the minister and his wife are good to him. As time goes on, Yusuf lets down his guard and settles in. Allah gives him wisdom and knowledge and half of the beauty of all creation; he grows into an attractive man. But because he is so beautiful, the wife of the minister, Zulekha, falls in love with him. She tries to seduce Yusuf one day while the minister is out, locks the doors and beckons him toward her. Yusuf resists. He is afraid of betraying God, afraid of betraying the minister. Yusuf runs toward the door. Zulekha grabs his shirt, and it tears. And that is when the minister comes home. He finds Yusuf and Zulekha, tangled and panting at the door.

There is a scandal and there is a trial. Both Yusuf and

Zulekha accuse each other of assault. But Yusuf's shirt is torn from behind: incontrovertible proof that he was being chased by Zulekha and not the other way around. He is declared innocent. How relieved he must have felt.

But Zulekha still wants Yusuf, and she gives him an ultimatum: either he sleeps with her, or she'll have him locked up. Yusuf refuses, and Zulekha makes more false claims against him. She uses her powers and money and connections, and this time, Yusuf goes to prison.

"What was that you were saying about Yusuf's story being about love and healing?" I ask Manal when she calls Wednesday morning. I'm sitting in a chair by my living room window, the blaze of the morning sun mirroring the anger burning in my chest. "This story is hard proof that love will fuck you up."

Manal laughs. "This part of the story is definitely not about love. Yusuf was a slave child in Zulekha's house. There was a major power imbalance in this situation. There's no way he could give consent. Whatever Zulekha was feeling, it definitely was not love."

"That's not what I mean. I'm not talking about Zulekha's love for Yusuf, I'm talking about Yusuf's love for Zulekha."

"I don't get it," Manal says. "He doesn't love Zulekha."

"Maybe not sexually, but he does love her. He loves them all: Zulekha, the minister, his adopted family, his community, his home. He gets comfortable. That's why this whole situation happens. He lets his guard down."

"Okay, I hear you," she says. "But what's the alternative? Never loving someone? Never letting someone get close to you?"

"Maybe? I don't know." There's a note of desperation in my voice that I'm hoping Manal doesn't catch.

"I don't buy that," she says evenly. "Let's say Yusuf never let his guard down. After the whole well situation, he decides he's never going to open himself to loving or trusting anyone again. Let's say he keeps to himself at the minister's and Zulekha doesn't try to seduce him and he doesn't go to prison. But then what? He trades pain and betrayal for loneliness? For never experiencing intimacy or connection or feeling seen? You think that's preferable?" She pauses. "For *Yusuf*, I mean." Her side-eye is so loud I can hear it through the phone.

"I'm not saying that," I say, trying to match the casualness of her tone. On the inside, though, I'm panicking, my breath coming quick and shallow. I take a sip of water to steady myself, to slow down this conversation I wasn't expecting to have, to dig up my usual snark from wherever it has disappeared to in the recesses of my body.

"Listen, Manal. I get that Yusuf is making the brave choice or whatever, good for him," I say. Manal snorts. "I'm just saying that staying open to love is not some magic bullet that makes abandonment issues disappear, okay? It's not like being loved by Zulekha makes him feel seen or connected. It's not like a lifetime of being left is going to be cured overnight just because there's love in his life, like he's suddenly going to be okay being vulnerable and messy. I hate when people expect that of you. It's not that easy . . ."

for Yusuf." I trail off, feeling exposed at having shared so much. At least I don't miss the irony.

Manal doesn't say anything, just lets me sit in my thought spiral. For someone who's not afraid to say what she thinks, she also knows when quiet is called for. Yet even as my relationship with Manal has grown deeper, more connected, I still find myself battling the instinct to hold back. Sometimes I still deflect answering *how are you*. I intellectualize the messiness of what I'm feeling about the verses, my doubts and my sadness, into discussions about the material consequences of rulings. I don't tell her, or any of my other friends, when they say things that hurt me, preferring to wait for the feelings to dissipate over having conflict. I'm so unused to sharing hard things that when my cat dies suddenly, I don't tell any of my friends. I'm too embarrassed about my grief—how raw it makes me feel—and eventually I swallow it, burying it deep. It's why flirting with straight girls was so appealing to me. Their leaving was inevitable, so I never had to let them in.

But Liv. Liv, whom I've been dating for a little over two years now. Liv notices, she sees it all. "Why won't you let me in?" she asks. "I'm here," she says over and over in a million ways—when she bakes cookies, does the dishes when I'm overwhelmed, and puts air in my bicycle tires because she knows the sound the gauge makes when it's fitted incorrectly stresses me out. "Let your guard down," she says to me. "Don't hide your face when you cry. Do things that are embarrassing. Dance." But I can't. I'm too scared to let people in. Too scared that they'll have to leave.

IV.

For the second time in his life, Yusuf leaves his home, his community, everything he knows—this time because he's going to prison. A familiar story today: an innocent young man incarcerated because of unsubstantiated accusations, because it's convenient to house him in prison, because he's poor and powerless and has nowhere else to go—what better argument for prison abolition? It is entirely unjust, but Yusuf is sent to prison. There he befriends his cellmates, interprets their dreams, and teaches them about God. The years pass slowly, but they pass.

A decade goes by and the king of Egypt has a dream that no one can interpret, in which seven fat cows are eaten by seven lean ones. Yusuf's old cellmate, who has since been released, remembers that while he was in prison, Yusuf had interpreted his dreams. He visits Yusuf in prison, tells him about the king's dream. Yusuf interprets it to mean that Egypt will have seven years of bountiful produce, followed by seven years of difficulty; that the kingdom should store food produced in the years of plenty to feed people in the years of scarcity. The former cellmate relays Yusuf's interpretation to the king, who is astonished; it's the first interpretation he has heard that is compelling and practical. He pardons Yusuf, clearing his name and exonerating him of the false charges, and, wanting such a valuable mind close by, invites him to be a trusted member of his cabinet. Yusuf agrees, on one condition: he asks to be in charge of the granaries.

"I know exactly what Yusuf is doing," I tell Manal when I call the following Wednesday.

"What is he doing?" she says. "Tell me."

"Yusuf knows that storing and distributing grains will become an essential job, during both the seven bountiful years and the seven lean ones. It'll make him one of the most important people in the kingdom. He's making himself invaluable. That's . . . that's queer indispensability."

"Queer indispensability?" Manal asks.

"It's a concept I heard about at a play I went to a few months ago—a solo performance piece by a queer Sri Lankan trans man," I tell her. "At one point, he talked about something he noticed, not only in himself, but in his queer friends and community—this way in which queer people tend to make themselves indispensable in their relationships and friendships. They're so afraid of being left that they make themselves unleavable."

"Okay," she says, but she sounds unconvinced.

"So, the person in the show, for example. He was talking about how, growing up, he was always afraid that his parents would disown him if he came out. And the way this played out in his future relationships was that he would try to be really, really, really good to his friends and partners—he would be there for them, do things for them, basically create reasons for them not to leave him. You know?"

"Sort of?" she says, but there's a gap between the way she's responding and the way this concept of queer indispensability gutted me that day in the theater, still guts me to this day. And I know, I know why she doesn't get it—it's because I'm intellectualizing, I'm not telling her how I cried that night, quiet hot tears that I hid from the friends I was sitting next to. How my entire being seemed to implode, how I held every muscle tight to silence my sobs. How shocking and overwhelming this recognition felt.

I decide to try again with Manal, this friend I love, whom I want to let in. I take a deep breath. *Be brave,* I tell myself. *Like Musa. Like Asiyah. Like Maryam.*

"Here's how it plays out for me," I say, my voice faltering at first, but growing stronger as I go on. "I've been so afraid for so long that I will lose everything if I come out. I've spent decades living on the brink of this loss—of my family, of my friends, my Muslim community. This feeling lives in my body. It makes me want to do everything possible to prevent this loss in relationships that I can—or think I can—control. It makes me make myself invaluable. It's why I glorify self-sufficiency, have a hard time asking people for help. It's why I minimize my own needs so I can spend all my time and energy taking care of others, so they love me, so they won't leave me. It's a way of making myself indispensable. It's a way of making myself unleavable."

I pause to take a deep breath. It feels good to be admitting this, better than I would have ever thought. I want to say more, to tell Manal about the many ways I make myself unleavable: listening to friends process their feelings for however long they need, even when I'm exhausted and sleepwalking between work and bed. Offering to water their plants and feed their pets while they're gone. Staying overnight with them during breakups. Keeping them company before doctor's appointments. Organizing birthdays and meal trains and baby showers. I want to list all these things for Manal, but in the easy silence that follows, I know she knows.

And the truth is also that l love doing these things because I love these people. But in the quiet before Manal responds, I feel confronted anew with the flip side of this way of being with other people—a way that's based in fear of people leaving, that prevents me from asking things of people in turn. That makes me recoil when others try to be there for me, even when I don't ask. That prevents me from being vulnerable, setting up a double standard where I'm convinced that vulnerability is a repellent in myself but not in others. I cried in that dark theater for myself, for decades of friendship where people were closer to me than I was to them, for this person I've become who wants more out of relationships, who wants intimacy and interdependence, who can only give but can't receive. Who is too scared to risk anything and everything, for fear of being left.

"Thank you so much for sharing," Manal says as I breathe out. "I know it must have been hard to tell me all of that."

I nod, forgetting for a second that we're on the phone and she can't see me.

"And I can see why you'd recognize that in Yusuf. I can see why that would resonate with you."

"Yeah," I say, because it's too hard to say thank you for this moment, this tiny little step toward a deeper friendship.

We talk a little while longer, and then we both have to get ready for work.

"Talk to you next Wednesday?" I say, because it's too hard to ask *are you going to leave me? Now that you know these messy things about me?*

"As if I won't start texting you memes as soon as we hang up," she says. And she does.

V.

Yusuf becomes the head of the granaries and makes himself indispensable to the kingdom of Egypt, establishing a reputation as being fair and kind. A few years in, Yusuf lets his position go to his head at least a little. I can see the temptation: he has the most important job in the land, after all.

One day during the seven lean years, a group of men come to Egypt. They have traveled from afar and are starved, with very little to trade for food. It's been decades since he last saw them, but Yusuf immediately recognizes this group of men as his brothers. They don't recognize him, though; they think he's dead, and the last time they saw him, he was still a little boy. Yusuf doesn't tell them who he is. He gives them their shares of grain and trades with them generously, as he would with anyone else. But then they ask Yusuf for an extra share for their brother at home, and Yusuf, who is in the position of power for the first time, pauses and then says no, refusing to give them extra food until they prove the existence of this other brother.

The thing is, Yusuf knows exactly who this other brother is. It's Benyamin, Yusuf's younger brother, his childhood playmate, and the only one of his brothers who didn't come along when the ten older brothers brought Yusuf into the desert. Yusuf guesses correctly that in his absence, Benyamin has become their father's favorite, the son who their father will now not let out of his sight. The brothers can't afford to forgo the extra share of food, so they return home. They ask their father to trust them with Benyamin, that they'll take him to the granaries to get more food and they'll bring him right back. "Like you did with Yusuf?" their father asks. He is wary, but they've been hit hard by the famine and eventually, he relents.

When Yusuf finally gets to see Benyamin, he is filled with love for his brother. Yusuf hatches a plan. He asks to speak to Benyamin privately, and reveals himself as his lost brother, tells Benyamin to go along with whatever happens next. Meanwhile, a cry goes up: "A thief! A thief!" The king's golden measuring cup has been stolen. "It wasn't us," the brothers say. "Check our things." The cup turns up in Benyamin's bag, where Yusuf has placed it while no one was looking. The brothers are aghast. They've sworn to their father that they'll bring Benyamin home, but now Yusuf gets to keep the thief as a slave, in accordance with the rules of the land. The brothers go home without Benyamin to tell their father, who's already lost one favorite son, that now he's lost another.

And just like when he asked to become head of the granaries, I know exactly what Yusuf is doing. He's testing his brothers.

"What do you mean, testing them?" Manal asks on the phone the next week.

"You know. He's testing them. To see if he can trust them again."

The brothers fail the test miserably. They say that if Benyamin has stolen, it's only because they used to have a brother Yusuf who stole, a brother who went rogue and left the family. Of course, they don't know they're speaking to Yusuf, that Yusuf planted the cup, that Benyamin is in on the plot. They don't even know that they're being tested. It's an unfair test, one they're destined to fail. And it's unfair of Yusuf, no matter how justified he feels, and I know this because I do this, too.

I test people unfairly all the time: like Liv, when I need to talk to her about a difficult situation I'm embroiled in. It's late and we're both reading in bed, and I'm panicking about the situation, having a hard time controlling my racing thoughts about worst-case scenarios. It feels like a huge vulnerability to ask her to listen.

"I don't have capacity to be empathetic right now," she says. "Can we talk in the morning?"

"Yeah, of course," I say. "No problem at all."

You shouldn't have asked, my brain tells me. *You've gone decades without being in a relationship. You don't need her; you know how to take care of yourself.* I quiet my thoughts and make myself go to sleep.

The next morning, I wait for her to ask me what I wanted to talk about. But she doesn't. She's busy with a work deadline and the whole day ticks by without her asking.

If she doesn't ask within forty-eight hours, it's because she doesn't love you, my brain says. *Probably because you haven't done enough to make her love you.*

She's going to leave you, I think about a hundred times a minute starting around hour forty-five. When the voice in my head starts to get so loud that I can't think any other thoughts, I march up to Liv, who is engaged in the deeply loving act of prepping our lunches for the week.

"Hey, Liv," I say before I can change my mind. "How come you didn't ask about that thing I wanted to talk to you about two nights ago?"

"What thing?" she says, looking confused.

Then, we fight.

"How could you not remember?" I say. What I mean is, *I needed you. It was so hard for me to ask.*

"Why did you wait so long to remind me?" she says. She means, *Let me in. Stop testing me.*

But I can't seem to stop. I ask Billy for help editing an essay and he doesn't get back to me in time for the deadline. Clearly that means I can't trust him to be there for me, that I haven't done enough to earn his love.

I test my family. Can we go an entire phone conversation without my parents asking how I'm doing, without them noticing that I haven't shared anything about my life? The answer is yes. We talk about the weather. We talk about my brother. We talk about what my mother has cooked for dinner. And they don't ask about me, which means I'm not important to them, that I should distance myself, that I should never expect emotional support from them, that they don't love me. An especially unfair test since I've spent years deflecting their questions about me and my life.

I know it's fucked up. I know that my mind is jumping to conclusions that don't necessarily follow from the evidence, that I'm actually gathering proof for conclusions I've already drawn. I know that this is self-protection, that I'm leaving before I'm left. And I know this is unfair to the people who love me and even to myself, but I just can't seem to stop.

"But what would happen if you stopped testing people?" my therapist asks. "What if you stopped for a month and pushed yourself to simply ask for what you need?" What would happen is that I can't. I can't imagine what it would be like to stop, can't unthink the spiraling, can't even think of the language I'd use to ask. I'm too afraid of taking without giving, which would mean that I'm no longer indispensable to people, that *they're* indispensable to *me*. And if I'm not offering or providing anything, people would start to notice they don't need me. But I need people to need me so they won't leave. I can't stop. I hate that I do this, I hate this about myself, and I hate this about Yusuf.

"Don't get me wrong: I'm not condoning the testing," I tell Manal. "Yusuf essentially kidnaps Benyamin to get back at his brothers. We're just supposed to assume that Benyamin is fine with being taken away from his entire family. And when their father finds out that his beloved Benyamin is now a slave, he cries until he goes blind."

"It's more complicated than that," she says. "Yusuf's hurting. He's trying, in his own way, to heal."

I am unconvinced, even though I want so desperately to be convinced.

"Why are you being so kind to Yusuf? When he's being such an ass?" I say. Despite the defiance in my tone, I'm gripping the phone so tightly my hand is shaking, and as I wait for Manal to respond, I hold my breath, hoping for compassion for Yusuf, hoping for compassion for myself. And my beloved friend delivers.

"It's you who needs to be kinder to Yusuf, Lamya. It all works out in the end. Yusuf tells his brothers who he is. Everyone apologizes to each other, and everyone forgives each other. Yusuf is beloved not just to his family but to the king, the people of Egypt, his community, everyone. He is no longer the little kid left in the well. He's the head of the granaries, yes, but his most important role winds up being a beloved member of this community—once he decides to let his family love him back, even if they're flawed and failing his tests. Once he lets his guard down, once he stops being blind to all the ways everyone is already showing him love. I mean, Yusuf's father is so happy to be reunited with his son that he gets his eyesight back. This love everyone has for Yusuf is real. He's not going to be abandoned again. It's time for him to let himself feel loved, not for being head of the granaries or interpreting dreams or helping people but for being Yusuf, their brother, their son, their trusted friend."

Manal has to hang up soon after to finish prepping for a class she's teaching, but I linger in my spot by the window for a little while longer, her words still reverberating in my mind. If she can be so kind to Yusuf, why can't I? Why can't I be kind to myself?

My glance falls to the slice of banana bread Liv has quietly placed beside me because she knows that I get wrapped up in my conversations with Manal and forget to eat. On the table in front of me is a get well soon card that my friends all signed when I had surgery—which I wasn't going to tell anyone about, but the hospital wouldn't let me leave by myself and Liv was working so I called Billy. And then of course, everyone had found out, had insisted on visiting, on organizing meal trains and bringing coloring books and hanging out, even though I had objected, had said I was okay. Tucked behind the bookshelf to my right, I see the various signs I've made for protests I've gone to with my community. Where people had insisted on staying close and protecting me because I could lose my visa status if I got arrested, had checked in with me at the beginning about what I needed, had checked in with me at the end of the night to make sure I got home.

Haven't I been loved even when I couldn't see it? By Liv, who cooks elaborate meals for me during Ramadan, is my backup iftar buddy in case everyone I'm supposed to meet up with bails. By my friends, who read the Quran with me and mentor me. Who remember that I'm vegetarian, who remember that I don't like hugs. By my community, in which people organize Netflix parties and workouts on Zoom so that we're in touch regularly even when folks have moved away, in which people send solidarity texts and messages when the world is too much. Isn't all of this love? Even when I haven't provided anything in return? Doesn't this mean I've needed people, and they've let me need them, and they're still, miraculously, here?

As I bite into the banana bread, I realize if all around me is the evidence of what happens without my asking, doesn't that mean that there's possibility for more? A more trusting love where I could let myself ask for things, let myself be vulnerable and imperfect and even dispensable? A more magnanimous, forgiving kind of love where sometimes people give me what I ask for and sometimes they don't and it's okay? Where it's okay to be disappointed and it's okay to be disappointing—where we can love each other and ourselves regardless?

Manal's words from our conversation earlier still ring in my ear. Yusuf is no longer the little kid left in the well.

And neither am I.

HAJAR

I.

This is a story about Hajar. A woman, specifically a Black woman—more specifically, an enslaved Black woman. A handmaiden in the house of an important prophet, and beautiful and beloved and wise.

There are other characters in this story. Sara, the owner of Hajar. Ibrahim, Sara's husband, aforementioned important prophet. Ismail, a boy born to Hajar and Ibrahim. But this story, my story, is about Hajar.

Sara and Ibrahim have had a difficult life. They've survived trial after trial: they've been expelled from their homes for believing in God, thrown into a fire by their enemies, fought tyrants aplenty, but their biggest trial yet is that they are childless. They want a child desperately—a child they can raise together, who will take care of them in their old age and carry on their lineage. They've prayed to God and been patient. They've cried and beseeched the Divine in a duaa immortalized in the Quran, *My Lord, grant me [a child] from among the righteous.* And still, no child. Sara and Ibrahim grow old. The years pass, their hair grays, and month after month, year after year, they remain childless.

After decades of trying, Sara has an idea: she offers Hajar to Ibrahim.

This is where the story gets murky.

What does being offered entail? How can someone who is enslaved offer consent? Is Hajar freed from enslavement and then offered in marriage? Is she being offered for rape? As a surrogate? As a co-wife? And Hajar, does she get a say in this? Does she even want to have a child, or be a mother? Is she scared or excited or nervous? Like Maryam, is she angry at her fate being out of her hands?

Sara offers Hajar to Ibrahim and, whatever it is, this murky arrangement, it works. A baby is born. A miracle, a boy, unexpected and late in life for Sara and Ibrahim, this child that they've yearned for. They name him after their yearning, Ismail, meaning "heard by God," this God who hears their prayers and gifts them this child, their child. Born to Hajar—a woman, a Black woman, enslaved.

Sara becomes jealous. Of course she does. She finally has this baby, a source of infinite joy that she's wanted and awaited and yearned for. But he's not hers alone. Hajar is there, too, holding, feeding, molding Ismail—a constant reminder of Sara's inadequacy. Sara feels left out, watching Hajar and Ibrahim with this baby.

Sara confesses her feelings to Ibrahim, pouring out her sorrows about how she didn't expect it to be this hard. She's not asking Ibrahim to fix it, but he decides he will. He decides that the best solution is for Hajar and Ismail to leave.

This is a story of a journey.

Hajar and Ismail and Ibrahim: a mother, a newborn baby, and his father. Two of the three exiled from their home, one escorting them to their exile while also doing the exiling, a measure that's not clear was even necessary. Three dusty figures traveling through the desert, away from their home. A journey under the scorching sun and across barren land, no one and nothing for miles. There is nothing in the Quran or Hadith about this part of the story. How did they traverse thousands of miles in the desert without dying? Did they walk? Ride horses? Camels? Join a caravan? Did they know where they were going? Did they have a compass? Did they navigate by the stars? What did they carry? What did they eat? How long did it take? Did Hajar and Ibrahim talk? What did they say to each other? Or did Hajar speak only to the baby, rocking him in her arms, whispering to him in soothing tones?

What was Hajar thinking during the journey, this enslaved person with no control over her life? What was she feeling? Was she afraid? Angry? Resigned to her fate? What was Hajar's experience of this journey to the middle of the desert, through a desolate landscape, this journey of exile with no destination, to no one and nothing but sand and rock and sun?

II.

This is a story about us.

It starts with a journey. A bus that we take together, Liv

and me. Well, the subway first, from a work party that runs a little late. A sprint to the subway and a mad dash down the station stairs. We pace along the platform, waiting for the train that has promised to arrive in one minute for the last four minutes. It finally pulls in, and we push our way into the crowded car, bags in tow, panting hard as we're held momentarily by the train's dispatcher, then *excuse-me-excuse-me* our way out of the car at our stop and run up the narrow stairs and out of the subway station. I race to the bus station to buy our tickets and then stand in the bus door to stall the driver, while Liv slowly follows behind, dragging our bags. She makes it to the bus a minute before our scheduled departure, but the luggage compartment under the bus needs to be opened back up to stow our bags. The driver slowly gets out of his seat to help us. Everyone on the bus collectively groans.

We make our way down the aisle as the driver starts the bus's engine. There are only two seats left, but they're far away from each other. We're both usually too nonconfrontational to ask someone to switch spots, but the prospect of six hours next to a stranger in the stops and starts of Friday evening traffic overrides my shyness and before I can chicken out, I ask the guy next to me if he would mind switching seats. "Yeah, no prob," he says, polite and unperturbed. Liv scrambles over with our giant bag of snacks and we spend the next few minutes catching our breath, settling our stuff, and sending frantic texts to say we made it onto the bus. *It's going to be okay,* Billy texts me. *Let me know when you get there safely.* Finally, finally, we're moving. Away from the city and finally en route, on this journey to the middle of nowhere and nothing but trees and fields and houses, on this journey to visit my family together, for the very first time.

I've been telling Liv stories about my family for years: my uncle who picked me up from the airport the first time I came to this country more than a decade ago; my grandma, who moved three years ago from the country I was born in to live permanently with my uncle; three aunts, another uncle, and three cousins, aged ten, twelve, and fifteen. These people I got to know when I moved to this country for college. Who nevertheless call me their own, call me every week to check in on me, send regular updates to my parents across the ocean to confirm that I'm alive. These people with whom I spend all my holidays—when I'm not playing hooky with straight girls from my Islamic center. Who never fail to send food back with me when I visit, or yell at me when it's been too long since I've seen them. I didn't grow up around them, but it turns out I didn't need to in order to feel like I belong.

These are the stories I've been telling Liv: about the shenanigans my cousins and I get up to on my weekend visits, the games we play and the pranks we pull and the food we eat, my valiant attempts to inculcate them with anti-oppressive values. The ten-year-old who is the most af-fectionate child I know, who follows me around and waits for me outside the door when I go to the bathroom; the twelve-year-old who is beginning to snark like the teenager she'll be in a few months, but who still wants to show me all her school reports and the books she's reading; the nineteen-year-old with whom I go on rambling runs, play cricket, talk about soccer; the grandma who makes my favorite dosas from scratch, makes and freezes vegetarian versions of meat-heavy food for me to take home. This family who loves me simply for being born to my mother, for being tied to them by blood.

I've been telling Liv stories about my love for these people and how easily they love me and fold me into their lives. And now we're finally on the bus and settled down and heading toward these people who love me, whom she'll be meeting for the first time, away from the city we call home and on our way to rural suburbia, to the middle of nowhere and nothing, on the night before Eid.

III.

This is the story of Eid, at least the one that gets told.

Eid al-Adha means the feast of sacrifice. Also known as Eid al Kabir, Qurbani ki Eid, and Bakra Eid, it has a multitude of names combining some variation of the words "great," "sacrifice," and "goat."

These are the characters in the story, at least as it gets told—in lectures at the Islamic center, in sermons, in Quran class at my school: a man, a father, an important prophet, Ibrahim. A beloved son, Ismail. Dutiful and obedient, destined to become a prophet as well. Born of a miracle and named after a yearning. Born to Ibrahim and Hajar, who is considered a side character in this story.

The story of Eid begins when Ismail is nearly grown,

still a child, but wise. Old enough to follow his father around everywhere whenever Ibrahim comes to visit Ismail and Hajar, who are both still in exile. Old enough to play and work, old enough to love his father deeply. And Ibrahim loves his son back. Ismail is the apple of his father's eye.

One day, Ibrahim has a dream where Allah tells him to sacrifice his son. Allah asks Ibrahim to kill Ismail. Ibrahim wakes up from this dream confused. Ignores it at first, tells himself that the dream must be the whispers of the devil, but then he has the same dream again and again, until he is rattled. He becomes convinced that this is what God wants of him, to slaughter his son like a sheep, like he sees himself doing in the dream: to tie him up and slit his throat.

Ibrahim tells Ismail about his dream, that he is being commanded by God to kill him. Ibrahim asks Ismail what to do. This child, who (spoiler: does not die) will grow up to be a prophet, too, with infinite patience and bravery that I cannot imagine and could never muster, says these sentences that God relates in the Quran: *Do as you are commanded [father]. You will find me, if Allah wills, of the ones who are patient.* Do what you need to do, Dad; I have faith in God, Ismail says. Gutsy as fuck, this child.

This is where the story gets murky again. Where is Hajar in this? Does she know what they're plotting together, her son and his father? Does she get a say in this decision to kill her child, for whom she was exiled, who is all she has? Does Ibrahim share the dream with Hajar, too? Is she, too, of the ones who are patient? Or does she wail, cry, and rage at the fate of herself and her child?

Ibrahim prepares to do what he sees in his dream, this

act he's so convinced Allah is telling him to do. Ties up his child like a sheep. Lays him down on a stone. Unsheathes his sword and raises it to strike in the ultimate act of sacrifice.

This is where the story diverges and accounts differ. In many versions, Allah says, *Stop. Hold up, that dream was just a test. You intended to follow through and the intention itself was enough. You've fulfilled the vision, passed with flying colors, that's all that was needed, good job.*

In the story that I prefer, though, Allah says, *No, stupid, I never asked you to do this. Just because you saw something in a dream doesn't mean that you have to do it, especially if it's something entirely unreasonable, entirely against the principles of love and justice and everything I've taught you so far. I was testing you, Ibrahim,* says Allah. *But the test was to see if you'd use the intellect that I gave you, and you haven't. You've followed blindly. You've failed.*

In all of the versions that get told, however, the outcome is the same. Right at the moment when Ibrahim's sword is about to pierce skin, Allah replaces Ismail with a sheep, a real, live, bleating sheep. Ibrahim slaughters the sheep instead and Ismail is safe, a little disoriented but alive and safe with neck intact.

Joy abounds. Everyone rejoices, but I can only think about Hajar. In my imagination, she stands nearby and cries hot tears of relief and wrath. Of fury—not just at Ibrahim but maybe also at God. Then I imagine her wiping her tears and drawing a deep breath. There is work to be done: the sheep must be butchered, the meat cooked and distributed, and a whole feast organized for this joyous day, this day that

her son was spared. For millennia afterward, people will tell
the story of what Ibrahim did while doing as Hajar did that
day. Like her, they will butcher sheep, goats, and camels in
celebration of Eid al-Adha. They'll cook and eat a third of
the meat and distribute the rest to the poor in honor of this
great sacrifice. They'll tell the story of this father willing to
kill his son for something his God possibly didn't tell him
to do.

But no one will tell the story of the Hajar of my imagination. Whether she stood by, fuming, as she does in my mind,
or wailed in despair, or was even there. She is a part of this,
too, this woman, this Black woman, enslaved. But hers is
the story that doesn't get told.

IV.

This is a story of love and yearning, too: Liv and I are dating.
It's been two years since our first good dates and things are
going well. We fight, but we also listen to each other. We
disagree, but take time to hear each other out. It feels different from romantic situationships I've been in before, different from a lot of the bad relationships my friends have
been in. It feels healthy and stable—and hard, too, but the
kind of hard that feels like growing, like learning, like trying.
And in these two years that we've been dating, she's taken
me to meet her deeply loving, deeply flawed family. I've
spent Christmas and a week in the summer on a lake with
her parents and sisters. I've bonded with her nieces and gotten to know her family well. I want her to meet my deeply

loving, deeply flawed family, too. So I invite her to come visit upstate on Eid—not as my partner, but as my friend. "Are you sure?" she asks a million times in a million different ways. "I'm sure," I say a million times in a million different ways.

But this is the story that won't get told to my family when we visit: the truth of my queerness. More than a decade after coming out to Cara, to myself, to Billy's mom, to many, many friends, my family on both sides of the ocean still doesn't know that I'm queer. They don't know that I'm dating a woman, that I've been dating at all, that we've been together for two years, that we're talking about moving in together. To them, my hijab, my butch outfits of baggy jeans and flannel shirts, read as modest; my short hair reads as convenience; and my rants about men pass as angry feminism. When it comes to my family, my hijab is my beard.

It still feels unthinkable to tell my family I'm gay, these people I love, who manage to be culturally conservative and also give me shit about my practice of Islam at the same time. They don't understand why I wear hijab, and have been giving me grief about it for years. "You know it's not in our culture to wear it, right?" my grandma tells me. "But it's important to always wear loose clothes and a dupatta over your chest. Anyway, you look so pretty without your scarf." My aunt says I look like a servant in hijab, not even trying to hide her classism. And they don't try to hide their Islamophobia, either. They try to convince me that wearing hijab is incompatible with "modern" values, that by choosing to wear it I'm refusing to assimilate and giving up all the opportunities that the United States can offer.

And also, whereas my family across the ocean doesn't speak of gayness at all, my family in this country uses words like "unnatural" and "mental health issues" to talk about queerness, and once even floated the idea that gay people might be possessed by jinn. "It's cultural," my uncle argued one evening when I visited for the holidays in my first year in this country. "There are no gay people where we're from, there are only gay people here in this country where people don't have the same family values." It's completely outside the realm of their imagination that people could be both gay and Muslim, could find freedom and power and solace in both queerness and faith. It's completely outside the realm of their imagination that it feels natural for me to love both God and this woman I'm bringing to meet them.

And this is why my story has to remain untold: I have everything to lose. I could lose my family's love, I could lose my love for them. I could lose the uncomplicated love of my cousins whom I've watched grow up. I could lose the big-hearted affection of my aging grandmother. And it's not just my connection to the only family I have here that I might lose, but also my connection to language and culture and food. Where would I go for Eid if they reject me? Who would I speak Urdu with, who would I watch cricket with? Who would I teach me to cook biryani? To improvise make-shift lotas, to do henna, to do these things it's taken me decades to embrace in this complicated process of unlearning that my culture and people are not inherently inferior? Who would I be without these things I love? I'm terrified not just by the magnitude of the loss but also of how easy it would be to accidentally out myself: one slip of the tongue, one unthinking moment, one wrong word.

I've lived with this terror for years. Even before I came out to myself and Cara, even when I was fourteen and crushing on my teacher, and maybe even before then, this fear has lived inside of me, smoldering. Over time, it's become second nature to deflect my family's questions with jokes or questions of my own, to redirect conversations toward their lives, to be careful to share very few details about my day to day.

But it's different for Liv. Her family hasn't always been supportive about queerness, but they've come around, and the scope of everything I have to lose is something she's never had to contend with. But she listens when I talk to her about it, she believes me and asks questions and listens, this white woman from Vermont with her own traumas around queerness. Side by side on this bus that's hurtling us toward my family, I ask again if she's okay with this, with the extensive rules we need to set for the visit—things that we can and cannot do in front of my family so they don't suspect that we're dating, to defend against my loss, to lessen some of our fears.

"It'll be hard," she says, opening a bag of crackers we'd packed. "But this visit is important to you. This is important for us. Who knows if we'll ever be able to see them without pretending to be just friends?"

I don't know how to thank her for the love in that statement, so I open a tub of hummus and try to get her to eat.

"We should decide on these rules," I say after we've put some food in our bellies.

"Okay. Definitely no touching."

"What? None? Can we at least high-five?"

"No way!" she says, aghast. "That counts as PDA!"

"Can I put my arm around you? Like a friend?"

"When's the last time you put your arm around a friend?" she asks.

"Maybe third grade?" I say. I'm not a touchy-feely person. Point made.

An hour later, our empty bag of crackers tucked into the back of one of the seats in front of us, we've collectively come up with an extensive set of rules. No sitting next to each other on couches, no pulling each other aside for conversations. No teasing or cuddling, even if we're in a room by ourselves. No inside jokes and, as I remember my first-ever bad date with the woman in the same leather jacket as me, definitely no stories punctuated with "we." No whispers, no stolen kisses, no sharing food, no sharing water, no nothing.

"It's temporary," Liv says lightly, squeezing my hand. "We're just going to switch off the romance for two days and become any old pair of platonic friends."

I squeeze her hand back and turn toward the window, unable to meet her gaze. My throat is constricted. These rules are an act of love. The wisdom of creating these rules and her willingness to put our relationship on hold are all acts of love. The playfulness and humor in her tone is an act of love. Our hiding is an act of love. This gesture of care and tenderness from Liv, on this journey to introduce her as a friend to a family who loves me, is all so beautiful and tender and unfair that I feel as if my heart will break.

V.

Here is another story that doesn't get told.

Before Ibrahim's dream, when Hajar is still a nursing mother, the three of them—Hajar, Ibrahim, and Ismail—reach the end of their journey of exile. They're in the middle of the desert, nothing around them for miles. No food, no water, no trees, no stream, no soil, no people, no reason for there to be people. A barren place with nothing but sand and sun and rocks. A nursing mother and her child, exiled by a man, a prophet in direct contact with God and beloved to the Beloved. A man who takes his child, a miracle child, a yearned-for child, and the woman who bore this child, to a desert in an uncultivatable valley and leaves them there. Alone.

"God told me to do this," I imagine Ibrahim telling Hajar as he sets off to return to Sara. "I don't know when I'll be back." I wonder if he had the decency to be embarrassed.

How Hajar responds is not recorded in the Quran, but in the oral tradition passed down through millennia of our mothers whispering. They tell us that Hajar says, "Okay. I trust in God. God will take care of us."

But my Hajar, the Hajar I imagine, seethes. She whispers under her breath: "I trust in God more than I trust in you, Ibrahim. Go ahead and leave us. God will take care of us more than you ever have."

In the version of the story that is recorded in the Quran, Ibrahim turns to the heavens before he leaves, raises his hands in prayer, and says, "My Lord. I'm leaving my family here in this barren valley, please take care of them, please feed them, please provide for them." This man leaves his child and a nursing mother in the middle of the desert, and turns to the heavens and prays to God. Makes duaa and then trusts in God. In the story that gets told, this man is extolled for praying to God and trusting in God.

But what of Hajar's incredible trust in God? The Hajar of my imagination, who chooses to stay. Who makes an active choice not to run after Ibrahim, not to follow him back home, not to wail and scream? Chooses instead to stay, alone in the middle of the desert with a nursing baby and dry breasts, no food, no water, nothing for miles. Chooses to stay not for a man but for God. Hajar, wholly trusting the Divine, with a patience and grace that I cannot summon when I hear this story in sermons, in Quran class, in lectures where this story is told. Where the story of Hajar, who chooses to sacrifice her home, her child, her life—for God and God's plan—is not told.

VI.

This is what happens on the Eid visit to my family with Liv: my uncle picks us up from the bus station and drives us to his home. It is almost midnight, but everyone is awake, waiting for us to arrive. They all come out to greet us, hug us, kiss us, welcome us like sunrise, all between the usual exclamations: Did you lose weight? Why don't you visit more often? Have you had something to eat?

And eat, we do, all weekend. Brownies and ice cream and soji ka halva in the morning: dessert for breakfast in my family's Eid tradition. Omelets for brunch brimming with jalapeños and haldi; rusks and chai and cheese. Lunch a few hours later: my grandma's vegetable biryani with potatoes cooked to perfection, beets that melt in our mouths. Between the five or six meals of the day, my uncle cuts us fruit. For dinner, my favorite chawal ki roti and jhunka. There's so much food that the cousins take pity on Liv and teach her how to say no when she's full: *tell Grandma you're going to eat more in an hour, list what you've already eaten, make sure your plate is never empty, make sure your plate always has a small amount of uneaten food.* Liv turns to me, full to the brim after second breakfast, and says, "I'm so angry, did you eat like this growing up? It's so unfair that you've gotten to eat like this your whole life, while I grew up on bland microwaved casseroles." I laugh and laugh and it doesn't matter that we're grinning stupidly into each other's faces because the rest of my family is laughing, too.

We do other things besides eating, of course. We play an elaborate camping game with the kids, build forts and pretend fires, with obstacle courses galore. We do a gross food challenge that the twelve-year-old cousin wins by eating a mixture of soy sauce and sugar and coffee grinds. We play a long game of Scrabble with my grandma that I win by playing a seven-letter word right at the end. All the cousins go for a walk around the neighborhood that turns into an impromptu hike when we find a hidden trail. Liv wears a nice shirt and pretty necklace to Eid lunch that everyone oohs and aahs over. As is tradition, they all try to convince me to dress up, but I refuse, somehow get away with wearing a clean, new T-shirt, while everyone teases me that my friend is rocking Eid better than I am. We go to Eid prayer—or I go, rather, with my one uncle who prays, to the Islamic center in the next town over. Stand side by side with people I don't know but feel connected to through this act, this morning prayer, standing before God to start the commemoration of this day of sacrifice. I cry through the dhikr that follows, these beautiful words that people are humming and chanting, thrumming through this room and thrumming through me: Allah is great, there is no deity except God, all praise belongs to Them; glory be to Allah in the morning and evening, praise to God in abundance, God alone we worship, to God alone we offer our sincere devotion.

There is more food after Eid prayer. Many of my aunt and uncle's friends visit, and we hold their newborns and make small talk about their vacations. In between, everyone lounges around the TV and hangs out. They've never met any of my friends and are fascinated by Liv, fascinated by her whiteness. They ask her all the questions they don't feel comfortable enough asking other white people: Why do white people wear shoes inside the house? Is it true that white parents don't care about their kids' grades? What do white people eat? My fifteen-year-old cousin plays YouTube videos by his favorite brown comedian about the difference between brown people and white people, beams at how hard Liv laughs at the skits. After second dinner, we pile into the car and go to the one ice cream store in town.

The next day, my uncle drives us back to the bus station and I'm as teary as they are when we say our goodbyes. Liv and I sleep through the bus ride back and then walk to the subway, our stomachs full of food, our bags heavy with enough leftovers to last us the rest of the week. We ride in a comfortable silence on this train we've taken so many times before. We don't need to discuss it, our bodies understand that she'll be getting off at my stop with me, join me at my apartment tonight, like so many nights but also unlike so many nights.

We alight from the subway in the city we love, buzzy even on a Sunday night, aglow in streetlamps and restaurant lights. A busker plays the drums in the park on my corner, and our footsteps mark the beat, seeming to echo back through the countless walks we've taken together from the subway to my place, echo back even further to when the footsteps were just my own, coming home alone from Eid and work and school and not-dates and bad dates and my first dates with Liv, until we reach my building. Finally, we're home.

VII.

This is what happens to Hajar: it all works out in the end. She is left alone in the middle of the desert in the middle of nowhere with a child, a hungry baby boy. No food, no water, no milk in her breasts. But my Hajar—this woman, this Black woman, enslaved—refuses to give up. Runs back and forth looking between two hills, searching for something, anything resembling life: a person, an animal, a sign.

This is where the story picks back up, the story that gets told. Baby Ismail is thirsty and angry, starts crying and pounding the ground with his small feet, and then God sends a miracle. A spring sprouts from the earth, water gushes from where Ismail's feet have been pounding, so much and so hard that Hajar sees it from the hill she's run to and sprints back to the spring, drinks from it, and is finally able to feed her son. Even after they are sated, the spring still pours out of the earth in such abundance that Hajar tries to control it, pours mud over it, says: "Zam zam." Stop, stop. The name sticks. To this day, that is what the spring is called: Zamzam.

And then, another miracle. A caravan passes by. Sees this woman and her baby alone, this miracle of water in the middle of the desert, and decides to stop and set up camp. The people in the caravan absorb the mother and the son into their midst, end up settling in this valley and living there for eons, and that is how the city of Makkah comes about. A city in the middle of the desert, near no one and nothing, built around this well called Zamzam, swelling around this woman, this Black woman, enslaved. All the result of an untold sacrifice, the sacrifice of Hajar.

It all works out in the end. God takes care of them, as God has promised.

VIII.

This is the story that will get told in my family: that time Lamya brought a friend over for Eid. How we all had a lovely time: we played games and ate and hung out with her and she was great, this friend. She was white but she fit in like she was one of us.

At the end of our trip, my aunt pulled me aside to tell me how much she liked Liv, how great it was that she did the dishes without being asked, that she tried all this new food, that she looked at photos of my cousin's wedding. "Bring her again," my aunt said. "It's clear that your friend is from a good family." I relay this message to Liv and she laughs and laughs and laughs; it's the most Muslim compliment she's ever gotten.

Here are the stories that won't get told to my family, neither the ones on this side of the ocean nor the ones abroad: all the sacrifices, big and little, mine and Liv's. The silence around queerness that made this visit possible, the years of omissions, hiding, deflecting, the layers and layers of calculations and carefulness and quiet. The love for my family that these silences spring from. And Liv, learning how to navigate my world, how to navigate how I navigate my queerness. The pretending to be just friends, the rules, the tenderness and care in her pretending. "It's just how life is," she says the night we return home, lying down next to each other in my bed, face-to-face. "These are the things you do for the people you love."

But these stories will be told between Liv and me—in words and actions. How deeply we love each other and the things we will do for each other out of love. These are the stories that we'll name and honor and cherish. In this new family we're building that's rooted in this love that, like Yusuf, I have trouble internalizing. That I'm teaching myself I can count on. That I'm teaching myself I can trust.

In the weeks, months, years that follow our trip, I find myself turning to the story of Hajar whenever it feels diffi-

cult or unfair or enraging to hide my queerness. I ask God,
the Divine Whom I love, Who I know loves me back, Whom
I trust with my entirety: Will You take care of me? Will You
protect me like You did Hajar? Will You raise a village, a
community around me like You did for Hajar? An ummah
of my loves, this family that I'm building with this woman,
with this chosen family of Billy, of Manal, of Zu, of my queer
Muslim friends, that I want to cultivate and bloom in this
city that I call my home? Will You raise this out of nothing?
It's for You, God, that I make this sacrifice. In You, I put my
trust.

YUNUS

"Really? Yunus?"

"Why not Yunus?" my friend Mitra says, somewhere between confused and annoyed. Our other friends are hiking
behind us in single file, so I can't see them, but I swear I can
hear them roll their eyes.

"I mean, just. Of all the exciting prophets to choose
from, it's Yunus who's your favorite?" I say.

A collective groan emerges from our friends. We're on a
camping trip—our first trip together outside of New York.
The idea of going somewhere had originated when I first
became friends with Manal, Mitra, and Reem the Ramadan
after the LGBTQ+ Muslim mixer. In the five or six years
since, we've acquired partners and best friends and expanded to a party of seven, including Liv. It's taken all that
time to make this trip happen, but excitingly, we're here
now, on a camping trip to a part of the country where none
of us have ever been: the wild, wild West.

It's day four of the trip, and we're on a hike to see a small glacier—"a hidden treasure," say the reviews on the park's website; "usually pretty quiet," says the woman selling us a map in the gift shop; "mostly safe but make lots of noise so you don't run into bears," warns the park ranger. We're now at the part of the hike that I hate the most. The views have been viewed, the glacier admired, the food eaten, and trash packed up. We're on our way back to our campsite, and all that is left is the trudging downhill through trails already traversed—somehow longer on the return.

Tedium is setting in, and with it, the threat of quiet, and with the threat of quiet comes the threat of bears. So I've decided to rouse us all by playing a few rounds of a game that I call "favorites," where there are no points and no winning, as requested by the group, possibly because of my extreme competitiveness. The game goes like this: we all take turns picking questions—What's your favorite fruit? What's your favorite number? Color? Tree?—and one by one, all seven of us answer. Passing judgment on people's choices is not supposed to be part of the game, but I've been doing it anyway. I'm tired enough that I've lost my ability to discern between acceptable teasing and pushing it too far. And anyway, these are some of my best friends and I know I'm not going to lose them over some heckling. Plus, they heckle right back, starting with the game itself. *Why do we have to pick one favorite?* Fine, pick three! *This whole idea of "favorites" is such a construct.* So what? Gender is a construct, too, but we play that game all the time. *Why do you get to decide the rules?* Because I'm a benevolent dictator!

I allow my subjects to go first, and now that it's my turn to pick a question, I'm looking forward to commenting on everyone's favorite prophet. Especially Mitra's choice of Yunus.

"No offense, but Yunus isn't that special," I say.

I guess everyone can tell that I'm about to go into full-on rant mode, because Reem pipes up from the back. "Lamya, is there any chance you can limit it to a few reasons you don't think Yunus is that great? Maybe pick your *favorites*?"

Someone slow-claps in the back and, despite myself, I laugh.

"Why, yes, I am absolutely capable of doing that," I say. "Reason number one: Yunus's big claim to fame is that he gets swallowed by a whale. And then the whale spits him out. That's his one big achievement, friends! He does very little else in the story. The whale is more prophetic than he is!"

I pause for dramatic effect.

"Another reason: Yunus essentially gives up. He preaches about Islam to his people, but they don't listen to him so he decides he's done and he leaves. He gets on a boat and sails away. He gives up!"

"That was two reasons; next prophet!" someone yells from the back.

"Who's your favorite prophet, Lamya?" Mitra asks.

"Maryam, of course."

"I thought only men could be prophets," Manal says from a few feet behind us. "Wait, that's my patriarchal in-doctrination speaking, isn't it?"

"Hasn't everyone heard that rant from Lamya?" Liv calls out, feigning exasperation but unable to keep the mirth out of her voice. "Maryam was definitely a prophet. Reason number one, God speaks to Maryam, which is a sign of prophethood; reason number two, God sends her a revelation, also a sign of prophethood; reason number three, there's some verse in the Quran where God is mentioning prophets and Maryam is included. Ergo, Maryam was a prophet, QED."

Liv's imitation of me is endearingly spot-on. Plus, it's pretty impressive recall for someone who isn't even Muslim.

"Who's next?" I ask.

We go down the line naming our favorite prophets. Or Greek Gods or leftist heroes for those of us who didn't grow up Muslim. I even allow a *no, thank you, pass,* from Reem, who doesn't want to answer.

The game winds down and we fall again into a comfortable silence. This hike is beautiful, obscenely so. A different kind of beauty from the sparseness of the desert where I grew up, a kind of beauty that I'm entirely unused to: greens so lavish, in so many different hues and shades, that my eyes hurt; the deep, menacing tones of the underbrush; lighter shades on leaves that have been bleached by the sun. And the blues: the water in the lakes, sparkling so majestically that I have to remind myself that it's real, that it's minerals and sediments reflecting light, not magic. The glaciers rising gloriously behind these lakes, views that I've only seen in thousand-piece jigsaw puzzles, in computer background photos. The trails lead us from vista to vista, through

meadows teeming with so many flowers and so much vege-
tation and life that our presence feels like an imposition.
"Hey, bear," we take turns yelling periodically into the silence, me more frequently than the others because I was
the only one who watched the national park's orientation
video and can identify the fresh scat we're constantly stepping over, stained purple with digested berries. "Just passing
through, bear! Thank you for sharing your home with us," I
yell into the mountains. I want them to know we don't take
being here for granted.

Just like we don't take each other for granted, Manal,
Mitra, Reem, and I. We were all displaced immigrants,
queer, Muslim, and different shades of brown, navigating
these identities alone before we found each other. A few
years after we became friends, Mitra and Manal moved
away from New York. But knowing too well the loneliness of
our lives without each other, we've maintained a firm com-
mitment to meeting up somewhere, anywhere, at least once
a year and spending a holiday or two together, carefully
building an infrastructure of constancy into our chosen
family. Now, finally, we're together with our extended fam,
the seven of us, hiking through this national park located at
the midway point between all of our homes.

This midway point also happens to be in a state where it
seems like everyone is white. The seven of us stand out and
elicit stares wherever we go. We're not exactly sure whether
these looks are out of intimidation or curiosity, but we're
unnerved enough the first day of our trip that we debate
sleeping with cooking knives in our tents. Most people

here—servers, cashiers, and park rangers—have talked easily and casually to Liv and Mitra's partner, the white people in the group, but won't make eye contact with the rest of us. They'll continue to direct their questions to them even when the rest of us answer. At one gas station, two men stare at us so aggressively that we get back into the car and drive to the next one.

But it's been worth it. We've managed to snag two campsites right next to each other, from which we can see the lake. We rented kayaks and spent a lazy afternoon floating on the water. We've admired glaciers, waterfalls, moose, marmots, elk, and bison. And of course, we've hiked, leaving our bodies tired and sore, stomachs ready for campfire meals, s'mores, and leftover pie from the general store nearby, making our sleeping bags feel extra warm and tents even more cozy.

The hikes have been the highlight of the trip, allowing us to spend time together as a group, but also hang out one on one. Like Mitra does with me, about a mile after the favorites game ends. She sidles up to me, links her arm through mine, and walks us a little faster to put some distance between us and the rest of the group.

"Aziz," she says, using a term of affection that never fails to move me. "I've been thinking. You're wrong about Yunus."

"I am?"

"Yeah. I think it's unfair to characterize him as a leaver. He left, yeah, but not before he preached to his community about God first. He argued and pleaded and tried to convince his people, to call them to justice. Yunus wasn't just a leaver. He was also a fighter."

I'd opened my mouth to retort before Mitra was done speaking, but now I close it, suddenly at a loss for words.

I've never thought of preaching as fighting. The trail grows narrower, and I concentrate on picking my way over slippery stones, Mitra's words churning through my head. I know she knows I'm thinking, that I'll respond when I'm ready.

Does it then follow that sometimes fighting is a way of preaching? Because I've been fighting for years. With a co-worker who called a massive flood in Bangladesh "natural selection"; a medical student friend who complained about a pregnant nonbinary person's use of they/them pronouns; a white roommate of mine who drunkenly told me that Islam needed to be reformed into American Islam so it wouldn't be run by "crazy people from the homeland"; an uncle who expressed nostalgia for colonialism; a cousin who advised me to move because there were too many Black people in my neighborhood; a friend who told me that gay sex is not real sex. I fought these people with all the ferocity, energy, and righteousness of my early twenties, feeling it was my moral calling. Sometimes I presented multipronged, well-researched counterarguments while speaking calmly. Sometimes I asked leading questions. Sometimes I yelled. I tried to contextualize my point of view in people's own lives. I wheedled, used humor, pleaded, cajoled, coaxed, produced evidence, begged. But not once was I able to change anyone's mind.

My fighting became a hashtag at work: every time someone said something problematic, my coworkers would call out "hashtag Lamya." Friends took to warning me before parties: "Lamya, I invited this guy who says some fucked-up things but he's a childhood friend, please don't fight with him." And in my family, my opinions were labeled extreme, crazy, feminist. As the years passed, I began to feel as if I was walking into every situation—school, work, my parents' home—already primed for battle.

"Okay, Yunus was a fighter. I'll grant you that," I say to Mitra eventually. The trail begins to widen and I don't have to step as carefully. I hear a few of our friends talking behind us, Liv's distinctive laugh. We're passing through a thicket of trees and I run my hands from bark to bark, inhale scents that I've experienced before only in candles and air fresheners. "But the thing is, Yunus still walks away from his fight. He gives up and leaves!"

Mitra stops to drink some water. "Aziz," she says when we start walking again, side by side. "What you're saying is true, but I'm trying to put my finger on why your characterization feels off. I think it's because Yunus's leaving is not the same thing as giving up. He knew when to disengage. He knew when to call it quits. He accepted that fighting was not serving his mission, was actually draining him of the ability to try and share his message effectively. His leaving was a way of taking care of himself. And it was also a way of taking great care with the message he believed in."

"But you can't just give up because it gets hard!" I protest. "Are we just supposed to accept when people say horrible, harmful things? I stand my ground. I don't give up." Even as I say this, I remember that I have stopped fighting with people as frequently and vehemently as I used to, but it's like my twenty-five-year-old self, desperate and full of rage, is crying out to be heard.

"Maybe not," Mitra concedes. "But you do protect yourself. Isn't that why you stopped fighting as much with people? Isn't that why you write under a pseudonym?"

Her words, spoken so gently, still hit me like a gut punch. My heart seems to stop beating for a moment—not helpful on this strenuous hike. Mitra is right. Sometimes it's annoying to have friends who know you so well. I speed up, as if I can outrun Mitra's point by putting distance between us on the trail.

But her words echo in my head nonetheless. It wasn't until I hit my early thirties that I finally admitted to myself that fighting was not working anymore. Not for the people I fought with, whose minds I never changed, but more important, not for me. Three years ago, a coworker said something racist about Black people and I fought with him until I was exhausted and he was even more fervent about his position. The next morning, I found myself unable to go into work. I sat on my couch, fully dressed, watching the buses I was supposed to be catching drive by, one by one outside my window. I loved taking the bus, I loved getting to work early before anyone else arrived. But the thought of sharing space with this coworker made my chest hurt and my limbs heavy, and I couldn't make myself get up off the couch. I felt drained of everything that makes life worth living: joy, energy, the will to go on. I sat there for an hour until I promised myself not to interact with anyone all day, until

I put on headphones and swore to myself I wouldn't take them off until I came home, even if I wasn't listening to music, even if anyone tried to talk to me. Needless to say, it was a very unproductive day.

That's when I decided to come up with a set of rules. I was never going to stop fighting for what I believed in, but I needed to fight differently. Only fight with people I'm invested in and care about, and who are coming to the conversation with genuine openness and curiosity. No fighting with casual work colleagues, frenemies, or friends of friends. Definitely no fighting with strangers on the internet. I resolved to ask myself, before engaging, whether I was being baited, whether people honestly believed what they were saying or if they were playing devil's advocate. I also decided to replace yelling with open questions, softness, vulnerability, and allowing for quiet, like Mitra is doing today on this trail—giving people time to absorb, reflect, consider. And I promised myself that if the conversation wasn't constructive, I would—like Yunus, I realize for the first time—allow myself, and them, the dignity of leaving.

And the rules, for the most part, worked. I learned to pick my battles. I learned to organize—fight collectively by planning events, protests, marches. And I began to write. Sick of being reactive, of standing up for my beliefs in these one-off encounters that only created further division, I took this new way of interacting—using questions, softness, and vulnerability—and brought it to the written word. There is an inherent quietness to reading that I hoped would create space for people to absorb, reflect, consider. Or, if they shared my views, to feel a little less alone in the crushing powerlessness of pointless fights.

This quieter form of fighting has offered me the ability to protect those things that make my life feel worth living. My heart constricts, suddenly, as I recall my fourteen-year-old self wishing to disappear, not yet realizing that my desire to die masked a deeper, more vulnerable yearning: my desperation to feel less alone. Using a pseudonym has made it possible for me to write about my experiences and help others feel less alone without putting my life on the line. Because even without opening my mouth to fight, I'm still a walking target and visibly different—a jinn, seen but unseen, a receptacle for the world's violence, ignorance, fear, and harm.

"Hey, bear!" I hear Liv shout. Mitra's footsteps sound behind me, soft and steady, peppered by the occasional crackle of a dry leaf or twig. She's right that I've learned to protect myself; my selective fighting rules have served me well on this camping trip, too. I've been able to ignore the staring and comments from the locals, stopping myself when I want to engage, argue, fight.

The latter especially came in handy when Liv and I visited her uncle for a night on our way to the national park. We were there to pick up the camping supplies Liv had brilliantly mailed to his address so we didn't have to carry them on the plane, but also because Liv wanted to meet this uncle, a complicated man whom she had avoided for ten years, who she was now afraid might die before she could comb his memory for stories about her beloved grandparents.

"Are you sure you're okay coming?" Liv asked for the

thousandth time the night before our flight, as we sat calculating how much toilet paper we should pack for camping. "He's really conservative and says whatever he's thinking."

"Yes!" I said. "I can handle it. We do hard stuff for family."

"But we could also just get a hotel and I could go see him for an hour or two."

"No, it's okay. I have problematic uncles, too. How bad can it be?"

It was bad—a different level of bad, maybe because life had been good to Liv's uncle for eight decades. He had made a lot of money and now lived with his fifth wife in a palatial house in a gated community. He picked us up from the airport in a huge truck, rolling right up to the curb below a No Stopping Anytime sign. He was clearly thrilled to see Liv, talking to her nonstop all the way home. I sat in silence, grateful for the break from interacting with people. It wasn't until we were at the house and two hours had gone by since he had picked us up that I started to notice how odd it was that he wasn't directing any questions or comments to me—that he had not spoken to me at all beyond our initial greeting. I began to interject here and there, but he wouldn't acknowledge that I'd spoken, and a few times, simply talked over me. *He probably didn't hear me,* I told myself. *He's probably going deaf. And he's probably just excited to see Liv.*

At dinner Liv's uncle finally addressed me for the first time. He looked at me and motioned to my hijab.

"So I'm guessing you don't drink, huh?" he said in a gruffer voice than he'd used all day.

"Nope," I said, caught a little off guard, food in my mouth.

"And you don't eat meat, either?"

I swallowed, trying not to choke. "Yes. I mean, no. I don't eat meat, I'm vegetarian."

Even sitting down, he was a tall, broad man, and he gave me a piercing look that made me feel as if I were shrinking to the size of a peanut. "That's just wrong," he said decisively. "Your religion is making you miss out on *all* the pleasures of life."

I was about to argue back when I remembered my rules. Liv lovingly squeezed my hand under the table and I exhaled, took another bite, and let the conversation drift back to Liv.

As the night went on, I noticed that it wasn't just me who shrank under Liv's uncle's glare—his wife did, too. One look from him during dinner and she would stop talking midsentence. At one point, he put his hand on her small wrist and she dropped the point she was making, instantly went quiet. He asked her to bring him more water, to grab a photo of his grandkids, to open the windows wider and cool down the room, and she did all these things with an urgency that looked like fear. The only person at the table he clearly adored was Liv. He said she looked just like her grandmother and invited Liv to his study after dinner so he could show her his gun collection. He filled and refilled her glass with expensive, aged scotch, even when she covered her glass with her hand and said she didn't want more. "Tell Liv not to protest too much about the liquor, hon," his wife said quietly to me as I helped her with the dishes. "Tell her she can just throw it out in the bathroom sink."

As the evening progressed, Liv's uncle got drunker and drunker and the room we were sitting in to watch TV seemed to grow smaller and smaller. Liv tried to ask about her grandparents, but every time she brought them up, her uncle would say he didn't remember and changed the subject. Eventually, he put on Fox News and turned the volume up.

"I have a Muslim friend," he announced to the room out of the blue, shouting over the blaring news. "He's one of the good guys, though. He's an undercover FBI agent, but he has a long beard and looks just like one of the terrorists. That's how he's able to catch 'em, you see."

He's provoking you, I reminded myself. *Count to ten slowly. Breathe.*

"I used to be a cop, you know," he continued. "Chicago PD, right after I graduated from high school, before I got into real estate. The stories I could tell you about Chicago." Then he launched into a series of tales about beating up Black folks, about "criminals" and people who had it coming, all his anecdotes sprinkled liberally with the N-word.

Liv started arguing with him, but her uncle only became more agitated, his voice growing louder and louder. I wanted to be anywhere but there, but also it kind of felt like I wasn't there anymore, like I was sitting above everyone, watching this scene unfold.

"I need some more water," Liv said after a few minutes, taking in my shell-shocked, terrified posture. "Lamya, do you want some, too?" I forced myself back into my body and followed her into the kitchen.

"Are you okay?" she asked once the tap was running at full blast. "He's always been bad but never this bad. I'm so sorry."

"He's not going to change his mind," I said. My eyes were on the steady stream of water, but all I could see was the door to his study, behind which lay who knew how many guns. "We have to stay here overnight. Please stop arguing with him."

When we returned to the TV room, we yawned loudly and excused ourselves for the night. *We have an early morning the next day, you know how it is, all the airplane travel tired us out.* I locked the bedroom door as soon as we were both inside, checked the lock a few minutes later, and then again before I crawled into bed and fell into a fitful sleep.

The next morning, we told Liv's uncle that we needed to be at the rental car place at 8 A.M., even though our booking didn't start till 10 A.M. I asked him lots of questions about his motorcycles just to have something neutral to discuss. An hour or so later, Liv's uncle dropped us off at our stop, but it wasn't until he turned the corner that I exhaled, that I felt like it was safe to be back in my body again, that I felt the blood rushing back into my limbs. The selective fighting rules had worked again, this time because we got to leave, alive.

I told this story to our group of friends as soon as we met them at the national park—pitched as comedy, an unforgettable encounter with Americana. What I didn't realize then was that Mitra—maybe all of them—hadn't missed the gravity of the situation, the self-protection that had allowed me to survive. On the trail now, Mitra passes me, my thoughts slowing me down, and as I watch her gingerly descending the steepest part of the trail, it hits me again that she's right. It's unfair to fault Yunus for leaving. After years of preaching, trying to convince his people with everything he has, Yunus makes the difficult decision to leave. God has promised that punishment is coming, and once Yunus finally admits to himself that no amount of energy will make it possible for him to convey his message, he decides to protect himself. Yunus gets on a boat, any boat, the next boat out of his coastal city, traveling somewhere, elsewhere, anywhere away from his community. This is where his story begins in the Quran, having decided to leave, embarking on a laden ship, undertaking this journey by sea.

After a few easy days on the boat, there is a storm. The sea is in turmoil, with waves as high as mountains, winds screaming and whistling, and clouds dark like the night. The ship is too heavy to bear this storm; it rocks from side to side and threatens to overturn. The people on the boat come together and decide: someone needs to be thrown overboard to lessen the weight, so everyone else can survive. The people are fair: they decide to draw lots to determine who needs to go. Yunus loses, not just once but a second time and then a third, and that is that: a sign from

God that it's he who must be thrown overboard. Yunus trusts God. Instead of being thrown, he jumps willingly into the churning sea, and as he sinks, a whale surfaces and swallows him. And then darkness.

Yunus wakes up in the stomach of this whale in the sea at night, alone and afraid. He doesn't know how long it's been or where he is. I've always been taught that the whale is a punishment from God for Yunus leaving his people, for giving up. But what if that's wrong? What if Yunus's leaving is not a giving up, but a disengaging to protect himself? What if the whale is not punishment, but protection? From God, from the storm roiling above and around him. From his people, who won't listen to him, won't listen to God. From fighting to exhaustion, from fighting to his demise. A brief respite, this whale. A shelter. A resting place. A protection, for the time being.

Just like my pseudonym—not giving up, not punishment, but rather, protection. A whale that allows me to keep fighting, to fight with my writing. A whale that allows me to save my energy for curious, kind dialogue and to support those I love—instead of fighting to fend off racists, sexists, homophobes, transphobes, Islamophobes who could look up where I live, where I work, who and what I hold dear. What if my pseudonym is a whale that allows me to build and love and resist through activism and organizing, these new forms of fighting that have replaced the yelling and raging of my twenties? A whale that is protection, for the time being?

In my whale, it's not lonely or dark. There are others

here, in this world I'm building for myself, people I have invited in: Liv, Zu, Manal, Billy, Mitra, Reem, and so many others. People whom I love, whom I fight with because I care about them. I'm building this world for people I know will fight for me, whom I fight alongside by marching at protests, fundraising for bail funds, organizing queer Muslim events that build community. In a way, my whale is akin to Hajar's exile—a seemingly barren, unfriendly territory that, with faith, can produce Zamzam, a spring around which grows a city. My whale is the city where God guides Muhammad, a place that feels like a homecoming after he's expended energy trying to convince those in power of the wahi. My whale is the little house with the garden where I imagine Asiyah growing old, her lover massaging her feet and braiding her hair. Sometimes people come into this whale, seeking protection or solidarity or a friend. Sometimes people leave because they want to engage differently. And sometimes we communicate in whale song—with others, in their own whales, in their own communities, fighting battles of their own. We send sonar signals that vibrate through the waves, traversing oceans and crossing worlds. Decipherable only to those who become very quiet, wait, and listen.

And sometimes, in our whales, we work on ourselves. Our own racism, sexism, homophobia, transphobia, Islamophobia. Our anti-Blackness. Our heedlessness around disability justice. Our defensiveness when called out. Our mistakes. We work on ourselves like Yunus, who calls out to God from inside the whale, turning to God in the prayer that he's most famous for: *La illaha illa anta subhanaka inni kuntu min athalimeen.* There is no God but You, Allah. Glory be to You. I have been of those who have done wrong.

Three days and three nights, Yunus lives in the whale. And then God tells the whale that it's time to spit out Yunus. God commands the whale to travel to a remote island with nothing and no one, and deposit Yunus gently onto the shore. God commands a vine to grow over Yunus, one that nourishes and shades him until he regains his strength, recovers, and makes his way back to his people. They have not been punished by the storm after all. His people have, in Yunus's absence, converted to Islam, have heeded his call to God, to good. They needed time and space to come to Yunus's words and positions before they adopted them for themselves. Yunus emerges from the whale into a better world.

This better world—that is the world I'm fighting for from inside the whale, this world I want to be birthed into. A world that is kinder, more generous, more just. A world that takes care of the marginalized, the poor, the sick. Where wealth and resources are redistributed, where reparations are made for the harms of history, where stolen land is given back. Where the environment is cared for and respected, and all species are cared for and respected. Where conflicts are dealt with in gentleness. Where people take care of each other and feel empowered to be their truest selves. Where anger is allowed and joy is allowed and fun is allowed and quietness is allowed and loudness is allowed and being wrong is allowed and everything,

everything, everything is rooted in love. And maybe that's an unattainable utopia. But I've found a few smaller versions of this world—in the ground rules Liv and I set on the bus en route to meeting my family; in the grace Cara showed me when I came out to her; in the patience with which Zu mentored me. I'm not naïve enough to think we'll reach this utopia in my lifetime or possibly ever, but I'm also not faithless enough to think that the direction in which I strive doesn't matter, that these smaller versions of the world aren't leading us there.

"I'm sorry for shitting on your favorite prophet," I tell Mitra, catching up to her as we approach the trailhead. "The prophet you named your bicycle after."

"Wait, Mitra, you named your bicycle Yunus?"

I turn around to see who's spoken and there, behind us, are my people. Five of my favorite people, and behind them rises the glittering glacier that we climbed up and around the side of a mountain to see, and above them birds are whispering to the big sky, and we're enveloped by the sound of my people talking and laughing and teasing each other for the various inanimate objects they've named.

"I just want you all to know: any more teasing about Yunus, and you're going to have to bake your own potatoes for dinner," Mitra says to the crew. It's her turn to cook tonight and she has promised us a feast of potatoes and beans and, somehow, fresh broccoli. Her partner is going to build us a fire, and Reem is going to drive outside the park to get us blueberry pie and ice cream from a roadside stand, and then we're going to make s'mores and play cards and talk into the night by the dying embers of the fire, and I can't wait for that feeling of sore muscles and feet freed from hiking shoes and full bellies and full hearts. This is the world fourteen-year-old me couldn't even begin to imagine. I'm already here.

ACKNOWLEDGMENTS

Julia Kardon, who somehow knew before me that I was going to write a book. For all the advice and for indulging my questions and for the crosswords. For having my back, always.

Katy Nishimoto, editor extraordinaire who made this book what it is. For reading thoughtfully, for pushing me in ways that allowed me to grow, for her brilliance in seeing how all the pieces fit, for always being up for solving my problems. For friendship.

Whitney Frick, Maya Millett, Debbie Aroff, Avideh Bashirrad, Andy Ward, Donna Cheng, Linda Friedner, Michael Morris, Michelle Jasmine, Cara DuBois, Susan Turner, Sarah Feightner, Rebecca Berlant, Leah Sims, Jordan Forney, and Andrea Pura at The Dial Press and Soumeya Bendimerad Roberts and Hannah Popal at HG Literary for believing in and championing this book. For all the hard work and heart they put into this project.

My mentors: Linda Villarosa, for making my first experience being workshopped productive and painless. For meeting me at 8 A.M. and giving me important advice. Naomi Jackson, under whose tutelage this book was conceived. For being an incredible sounding board and careful reader, for giving me the feedback—good and bad—that I needed to hear. Bushra Rahman, for paving the way and being the queer South Asian Muslim writer that I needed to see in the world. Saadia Toor, for telling me to channel my anger into writing. Serena W. Lin, for patiently teaching me "show, don't tell," for inspiring me to keep track of my rejections, for believing in me. Mariam Habib, for changing my life.

Lambda Literary and Queer | Art | Mentorship for their support, for connecting me to some of my favorite people. For being a writing home.

JO, EC, EB, MK, SD, FIC, SR, CC, NA, and RR for writing, reading, and editing with me throughout the years. For reminding me to keep writing and holding me accountable to deadlines.

My chosen family, my forever friends: JO, MH, EA, SD, FIC, SC, QD, LK, ACAB, OB, RR, TD, LS, SR, SG, HZ, JG, FA, EC, NA, ST, LW, MS, KC, SR, RM, and others that I'm going to kick myself for missing. For expanding my definition of love. Please never leave me.

My brother, for being there through it all. My cousins, for being my fiercest advocates and for teaching me to use emojis ironically. My family, for nurturing me.

JL, for loving me in ways that I could never have imagined, for the intentionality and tenderness and care. For B.

To all, my infinite love and gratitude.

ABOUT THE AUTHOR

LAMYA H is a former Lambda Literary Fellow whose writing has appeared in *Vice, Salon, Vox, Black Girl Dangerous, Autostraddle,* and the *Los Angeles Review of Books*. She currently lives in New York with her partner.

lamyah.com
Twitter: @lamyaisangry
Instagram: @lamyaisangry

ABOUT THE TYPE

This book was set in Fairfield, the first typeface
from the hand of the distinguished American artist and engraver Rudolph Ruzicka (1883–1978).
Ruzicka was born in Bohemia (in the present-day
Czech Republic) and came to America in 1894.
He set up his own shop, devoted to wood engraving
and printing, in New York in 1913 after a varied
career working as a wood engraver, in photo-
engraving and banknote printing plants, and as
an art director and freelance artist. He designed
and illustrated many books, and was the creator
of a considerable list of individual prints—wood
engravings, line engravings on copper, and aqua-
tints.